EVERYWOMAN HER OWN THEOLOGY

UNDER DISCUSSION
Marilyn Hacker and Kazim Ali, General Editors
Donald Hall, Founding Editor

Volumes in the Under Discussion series collect reviews and essays about individual poets. The series is concerned with contemporary American and English poets about whom the consensus has not yet been formed and the final vote has not been taken. Titles in the series include:

Everywoman Her Own Theology: On the Poetry of Alicia Suskin Ostriker
edited by Martha Nell Smith and Julie R. Enszer

Mad Heart Be Brave: Essays on the Poetry of Agha Shahid Ali
edited by Kazim Ali

Anne Carson: Ecstatic Lyre
edited by Joshua Marie Wilkinson

From Sorrow's Well: The Poetry of Hayden Carruth
edited by Shaun T. Griffin

Jean Valentine: This-World Company
edited by Kazim Ali and John Hoppenthaler

On Frank Bidart: Fastening the Voice to the Page
edited by Liam Rector and Tree Swenson

On Louise Glück: Change What You See
edited by Joanne Feit Diehl

On James Tate
edited by Brian Henry

Robert Hayden
edited by Laurence Goldstein and Robert Chrisman

Charles Simic
edited by Bruce Weigl

On Gwendolyn Brooks
edited by Stephen Caldwell Wright

On William Stafford
edited by Tom Andrews

Denise Levertov
edited with an introduction by Albert Gelpi

The Poetry of W. D. Snodgrass
edited by Stephen Haven

On the Poetry of Philip Levine
edited by Christopher Buckley

James Wright
edited by Peter Stitt and Frank Graziano

Anne Sexton
edited by Steven E. Colburn

On the Poetry of Galway Kinnell
edited by Howard Nelson

Robert Creeley's Life and Work
edited by John Wilson

Everywoman Her Own Theology

On the Poetry of Alicia Suskin Ostriker

Edited by Martha Nell Smith and Julie R. Enszer

UNIVERSITY OF MICHIGAN PRESS

Ann Arbor

Published in the United States of America by the
University of Michigan Press
Manufactured in the United States of America
Printed on acid-free paper
First published September 2018

A CIP catalog record for this book is available from the British Library.

Library of Congress Cataloging-in-Publication Data

Names: Smith, Martha Nell, 1953– editor. | Enszer, Julie R., 1970– editor.
Title: Everywoman her own theology : on the poetry of Alicia Suskin Ostriker / edited by Martha Nell Smith and Julie R. Enszer.
Description: Ann Arbor : University of Michigan Press, 2018. | Series: Under discussion | Includes bibliographical references. |
Identifiers: LCCN 2018019708 (print) | LCCN 2018021160 (ebook) | ISBN 9780472124404 (E-book) | ISBN 9780472037292 (pbk. : acid-free paper)
Subjects: LCSH: Ostriker, Alicia—Criticism and interpretation.
Classification: LCC PS3565.S84 (ebook) | LCC PS3565.S84 Z63   2018 (print) | DDC 811/.54—dc23
LC record available at https://lccn.loc.gov/2018019708

Cover photograph by Miguel Pagliere.

for Alicia

beloved friend, partner, lover, sister, mother, daughter, teacher,
singer, writer, critic, rebel, prophet. Poet in all.

> *And we are put on earth a little space,*
> *That we may learn to bear the beams of love. . . .*
> —WILLIAM BLAKE

Acknowledgments

Expressions of gratitude never quite seem to carry the depth, complexity, profound appreciations that drive one to utter them in the first place. We owe much to Marilyn Hacker and Kazim Ali, who believed in this project all along. Especially to Marilyn Hacker we are indebted for suggestions, arranging introductions and communications to some contributors, a keen deft sense of just how a book such as this could become a reality in the hand, suited for the beach, the park, the backyard, the den, the fireside, the bedroom, and her determination to make it happen.

To all of our contributors included in this volume you now hold in your hand, we can't thank you enough for encouraging readers to delve deeper into the amazing poetry of Alicia Ostriker. In fact, you intrigued and inspired the copyeditor to get all of her books and read her poetry.

To contributors who also submitted wonderful essays that are not in this volume, we appreciate you sharing some of your reflections on Alicia Ostriker and are proud to feature them here: http://aliciaostriker.com

Our warm thank you to Susan Cronin at the University of Michigan Press for shepherding the project; to Daniel Otis for the thoughtful and comprehensive copyediting; and to Kevin Rennells for the care and deft attention to the production process.

Contents

MARTHA NELL SMITH

Introduction

Alicia Ostriker Thumbtacking Her Theses
to the Bulletin Board

The epigraph and title for Alicia Ostriker's *No Heaven* (2005) are
from John Lennon's song "Imagine." When interviewing Ostriker,
poet Cynthia Hogue observed that the "notion of 'joy' seems to run
like a golden thread through" her oeuvre with such images as dogs
leaping into the surf "For absolutely nothing but joy," even as she
acknowledges that this is a "wounded / World we cannot heal" and
that "in this century / To survive is to be ashamed" (Interview, *in-
novative women poets* 261; "The Dogs at Live Oak Beach, Santa
Cruz," *The Crack in Everything*). Indeed, fierce, funny, philosophical,
astute, playful, sober, acute, relentlessly honest, faithful in observa-
tion, loving completely so that she is clear-eyed, direct, Alicia Os-
triker appeals to a wide range of readers—rabbis, scientists, other
poets and writers, literary critics, women waking up to their femi-
nist impulses . . . or not, men who are proudly feminists . . . or not,
humans in love, humans caught in hate or indifference, humans
searching, stuck, recalcitrant, obedient, rebelling. Intensely personal
and connected even as she is objective, rational, detached, Ostriker
and her poetry, all her writings, give and regive, hold one account-
able even as she gives one permission to be all too human, and of-
fers it, making clear that there really is no permission to give.

As I and then Julie Enszer and I were collecting the rich re-
sponses that comprise *Everywoman Her Own Theology: On the Poetry
of Alicia Suskin Ostriker*, I found myself thinking through my four
decades with her as mentor, as friend, as teacher always willing, al-
ways in fact seeking, to learn. Doing so, I found myself musing on
just how far women have come since she and I first met in 1977, and
how we constantly run the risk of forgetting how women's lives
have changed, and who was responsible for changing them—
women such as Alicia—and thus we run the risk of forgetting and
drinking backslider's wine, as it were.

Having already said she needed to go, Alicia would stand with a student—me—on the corner of College Ave. and Hamilton in New Brunswick, New Jersey, and listen to me spill out a painful, confusing coming-out story. Alicia listened conscientiously, staunchly there as a friend. I'd been disowned, cut off. She looked at me, listened to me, said, "You're going to make it. Get a job. Don't repay your parents in kind." She's the kind of teacher who asks, "Why me?" when I asked her to direct my dissertation on Emily Dickinson. "I'm not an Americanist," she said. "That's the point," I replied, "you do poetry." She then proceeded to tell me that my first argument for taking Dickinson's manuscript experimentations seriously seemed unlikely to be correct (the dashes dancing up and down), but why didn't I make her an argument that seemed credible? I did, and she accepted it as plausible, though she remained unpersuaded. She's the kind of mentor who'll sit with you on the floor of Special Collections in a research library poring over a collection the curators then had locked away—*The Manuscript Volumes of Emily Dickinson*. She's the kind of teacher who asked why wouldn't I want to send out my most provocative (explicitly lesbian) piece of writing when applying for jobs—she'd watched me work so hard to come out of the closet, why occlude that and not send out my best piece of writing? She's the kind of mentor who'll skip part of a conference with you to take a swim in the Pacific (in fact, she'll be the one who suggests it).

She is wise, and she is good, and she is full of the best sort of surprises, and was teaching the audacity of hope long before that was a political promise. At a spring 1986 reading in a New Brunswick bar so packed that listeners were craning in from the sidewalk outside, I was quite frankly astonished by:

A QUESTION OF TIME

I ask a friend. She informs me it is ten years
From when her mother wrote
"I hope at least you are sorry
For causing your father's heart attack,"
To now, when they are speaking
Weekly on the phone
And almost, even, waxing confidential.
I check my watch. Ten years is rather much,
But I am not a Texas Fundamentalist,
And you are not a red-headed Lesbian,

So it should take us shorter, and I should get
Time off for good behavior
If I behave well, which
I do not plan to do.

I was the "friend" in that poem, encouraged to have the audacity
to be myself—two simple words so easily taken for granted, yet
remarking the most powerful act, the only way each of us can step
into, or rather slouch toward, the divine state "I am that I am."
When as an assistant professor I read that those who had mentors
who published tended to do so themselves, I was thrilled. But I have
not been editing this volume with poet and editor Julie Enszer, and
you are not reading this volume, to hear about Alicia Ostriker's re-
lationship with me. But the way I am inclined to go on and always
in conversation will go on so when thinking about Alicia tells you
something about Alicia Ostriker in the world, Alicia Ostriker at
work, Alicia Ostriker at play, Alicia Ostriker in love, Alicia Ostriker
in friendship. Alicia is all about connectedness, connectedness to the
world and each and every one of us.

Preparing *Everywoman Her Own Theology*, I several times read all
of Ostriker's published poetry and published prose, and let me tell
you that is a treat I more than strongly recommend. Take Ostriker
on the plane, on the train, on the metro, take her on the bus, take
her to the beach—you will be abundantly rewarded time and again.
I also pulled every review I could find of Ostriker's work, and I was
deeply impressed with the great respect, the awe, that imbues all of
them, even those she has infuriated, pissed off. To Alicia I'll say, you
do that sometimes, Alicia, because you are direct and you say things,
say stuff that matters.

Reading assessments of Ostriker's critical prose, I was not at all
surprised that all other readers remarked incisiveness, perspicacities in
her very early work on William Blake that always related to larger
issues of his art . . . and ours. Sitting in Ostriker's seminar last millen-
nium I was reminded, as I am when reading her poetry, why I have
devoted myself to literature, to poetry—"[Hu]Man[s] have no body
distinct from our Souls." Was *that* the most important thing I learned
studying Blake with Ostriker, or was it—"Those who restrain desire,
do so because theirs is weak enough to be restrained"? Visionary,
energetic, rigorous, flexible, Ostriker more than understands the
practical and political aspects of poetry. Reading Ostriker's writings as
a woman, on writing as a Jew and reflecting on being a Jew, I took

heart, and I have continued to be buoyed over and over again by her courageous rereading of the Bible—rereading as bravely as did Emily Dickinson, rereading the Holy Book creatively, interactively, and from a fiercely relentless autobiographical perspective. Studying *Paradise Lost* with Ostriker, I saw what I might not have dared notice or have written pages about—Adam wilts in Milton's iambic pentameter as Eve asks, "Why *not* eat the fruit of that tree?" Eve, Ostriker taught me to see, introduced not sin, but critical inquiry into the world. No wonder when talking with Joan Larkin, who described watching her dance with the Torah, Ostriker observed:

> You're holding something very precious and dancing with it. And it was really different from how I usually see my relationship with the Torah, which is with words: words that I read, and that I wrestle with. I usually think that my relation to the Hebrew Bible is like Jacob's relationship with the angel, wrestling all night. I'm trying to wrestle a blessing out of it, and it's resisting, and we could go on wrestling like that forever. And that's me with scripture, with holy words, that from which women are so much excluded. But dancing with it, having that physicality, was just plain beautiful. [The interview immediately follows this essay.]

Reading Ostriker is dancing with Alicia, physical, spiritual, emotional, cerebral, and just plain beautiful. No wonder the late Maxine Kumin declared *The Crack in Everything* "Tough-minded, lyrical, passionate," noting that your "distinctive voice discourses on 'these rusty chains of being that bind us,' providing an overview of our dangerous era, singing what is." Yes, there is a crack in everything, and Ostriker repeatedly reminds us that that is how the light gets in, helps us, especially during these very dark days of our republic, "better understand our American selves," so that we stand with her and shout

> *Oh you can't scare me I'm sticking to the Union*
> for we believed a better world was coming
> such and such my sources and my spring
>
> for which I sink to my knees in gratitude
> and dare you my fellow citizens
> in the nation of money
>
> I dare you to mock me.
>
> ("Born in the USA," *The Book of Seventy*)

An eroding, "perplexed" America Ostriker has, in her ferocious honesty, called "this moon-shaped blankness" (*No Heaven* 109), a blankness on which she writes, giving us hope that our nation's erosion is not, after all, its immutable destiny. With Diane Middlebrook we clap and laugh with recognition, *yes*, Ostriker's poems "'hang in the air like Nijinsky taking a nap'—no need of heaven when the living can perform such feats." With Gerald Stern, we shout, *AMEN*, Ostriker **is** "a fool for beauty." Yes, she does say so on "'West Fourth Street.'" And *YES*, Ostriker is "also a fool for wisdom but, like a smart sage," and like my other mentor Emily Dickinson, she does "it slant." Jean Valentine is right—"*The Book of Seventy* will speak to everyone: Alicia Ostriker's honest voice, her humor, her wisdom, her gutsiness; her scholarly, longing mind; her knowing body: 'my mind is a cervix / I can imagine anything'; and from the first page to the last, her long-recognized courage in facing down—even welcoming—just about everything." And Marilyn Hacker is also on target when she remarks Ostriker's "compendium of learned, crafted, earthy, and outward-looking poems that show how this quest has informed and enriched her whole poet's trajectory." Yes, Blake is right, and so is Mark Doty when he proclaims of *The Old Woman, the Tulip, and the Dog* that the sequence "could only have been written by a poet who has both lived and written her way to this marvelously idiosyncratic, urgent, no-holds-barred book, a masque and pageant not to be missed."

In Ostriker's essay praising child rearing for putting the artist in touch with the factual world and with the hope that mothering might one day enjoy a prominence in literature equal to that of sex and war, the profundities abound in refusing to fear connectedness, mutuality, continuity, identification, touch, in declaring that the imperative of intimacy is political. In my own home, Alicia Ostriker has given us many a prayer for holidays and other special occasions, and all have been "practical and magical, strong wine and food time coming . . ." ("A Meditation in Seven Days").

When Alicia and Jerry (her astrophysicist husband) were interviewed by *Scientific American*, both noted that the cultures of science and the humanities are much more alike than C. P. Snow had bemoaned, and Ostriker observed the similar ways that ideas are created and tested: "first you know something intuitively and then you try to prove it. . . . If it turns out you can't prove it, then it's wrong. Writing a poem is much the same; you try to find the right words, and if you can't, you didn't really know the poem. . . . Insofar as real poetry and real science get done, they get done by people who, consciously or otherwise, are operating as part of the universe rather than separate from it."

In "Suite for Eleanor," published just when the *Women's Review of Books* had been rejuvenated in 2006, Ostriker wrote:

THE MOUNTAIN

Difficult to say what the supreme
Moment is in the life of a mountain,
But in your sixties when they made you a delegate

To the United Nations you pushed through
A finished draft of the Universal Declaration of Human Rights.
You insisted the phrase *all men are born free and equal*

Be changed to say *all human beings*,
You graciously forced the other delegates to compromise
With one another on wording. To get it done. And it was done.

Alicia Ostriker has always graciously encouraged me to get it done, not to bother with the creeps and the petty competitions, but to get it done, to treat myself well and focus on what's truly important. She has done that for everyone fortunate enough to read her, listen to her. Ostriker enables us to "Imagine there's no heaven . . . No hell below us, Above us only sky . . . Imagine all the people, living life in peace."

With *Everywoman Her Own Theology*, Julie Enszer and I give Alicia back her own epigram, taken from her beloved Blake:

For we are put on earth a little space
That we may learn to bear the beams of love.

("The Little Black Boy")

We give that back to Alicia Ostriker, who made this volume possible, and to all of *Everywoman Her Own Theology*'s contributors, some of whom quote her extensively, some of whom do not, but all voice deep appreciation of and indebtedness to the content of her deft, wise, courageous, loving poetic responses to the world and all creatures big and small. We begin with a recent interview with Joan Larkin, in which Alicia Ostriker's writerly evolutions, poetic vision, and hopes for her work and for poetry's work in the world become more and more clear as the conversation unfolds. In the words of Marianne Moore, Ostriker's work is "strong enough to trust to." To *Everywoman Her Own Theology*'s readers, we offer the "beams of" tough "love" that permeate these responses to Ostriker's work over the last fifty years in the hope that each and all will dwell in the possibilities afforded by the more numerous rooms, windows, and doors found in reading, and in reading about, Alicia Ostriker's work.

JOAN LARKIN

Dancing with the Torah
Joan Larkin Interviews Alicia Ostriker

Smith College, April 7, 2014

> JOAN LARKIN: I'd like to start by sharing an image of you that's left an indelible impression.
>
> ALICIA OSTRIKER: Oh dear [*laughs*].
>
> JL: No, it's a beautiful one! Last fall, I was with you at Romemu, the Jewish Renewal synagogue, on Simchat Torah. It was intensely celebratory—a day when we have the opportunity to hold the Torah and dance with it. I was feeling shy, just watching, but you were participating. I can't forget seeing you in the middle of the center aisle, wrapped in a white tallit and holding the Torah. You looked as if you were carrying a child on your shoulder, or cradling a lover. It was a very close embrace, but I could also see that the Torah was heavy—
>
> AO: —It is very heavy.
>
> JL: Literally, and—
>
> AO: —in every other way.
>
> JL: What did that feel like? Did it seem like a metaphor for your relationship to Torah?
>
> AO: That's such an interesting question. The history of Simchat Torah is that you're celebrating the end of the round of reading through the five books and beginning the new round. It's a moment of celebration, and you're supposed to hold it in your arms and dance with it and be completely joyful—and in most congregations, that's men. If you go to Williamsburg, say, to watch Simchat Torah being celebrated—and many tourists do—what you'll see is men crowding around, dancing, and being joyous, cradling the Torah in their arms—and the women are on the sidelines. When I had the opportunity to be part of that, I didn't know what it would feel like. I'd never done it before. I liked getting up in the aisles and dancing. I like dancing—you know that. And then the idea of holding it myself, in my own arms. . . .

Torah is a feminine noun, so you're holding something that's sacred and female in your arms. Whenever I've been to a service before, they'll walk around carrying the Torah, and you take your prayer book and touch it to the Torah and kiss your prayer book. It's all happening at a distance. So what this felt like for me—it was heavy, literally, and like holding a living being.

JL: It sounds exhilarating.

AO: You're holding something very precious and dancing with it. And it was really different from how I usually see my relationship with the Torah, which is with words: words that I read, and that I wrestle with. I usually think that my relation to the Hebrew Bible is like Jacob's relationship with the angel, wrestling all night. I'm trying to wrestle a blessing out of it, and it's resisting, and we could go on wrestling like that forever. And that's me with scripture, with holy words, that from which women are so much excluded. But dancing with it, having that physicality, was just plain beautiful.

JL: Were you feeling any undertone of anger about the patriarchal possession of the Torah, or was that missing from that moment?

AO: I was just wondering *How long do I get to do this before someone takes it from me?* Because one person can't hold it the entire time. You're supposed to share.

JL: Lots of people wanted that opportunity.

AO: So I did have to give it up, but the act was simply beautiful, exhilarating—because you're dancing!

JL: My sense is that you've been dancing with the Torah your whole life. Or to use your word: wrestling.

AO: Yes.

JL: The Bible is such an important part of your writing life and of your intellectual life and your poetry life. What were your first encounters with it?

AO: My first encounter with the Bible was not until I was in college. I knew almost nothing. I was raised an atheist socialist Jew, that special strand of Judaism. My religious upbringing consisted of being told that religion was the opiate of the people. But I was always drawn to the religious poets. I loved John Donne, I loved Gerard Manley Hopkins, and I especially loved the heterodox ones: loved, loved, Whitman, loved Blake. Something drew me in—something in the energy of spirituality in the poets I already loved. But I didn't know a thing about Judaism.

JL: The poets you've just mentioned are all Christian.

AO: Oh yes. In college my boyfriend, who was later my husband, suggested that I read the Bible. He said, "It's a good book, I think you'll like it." [*Laughs*]

JL: Wow. Praise to Jerry, I didn't know he'd done that.

AO: Yes. So I spent a summer reading through it, the good parts, the stories and the poetry. I skipped Leviticus; I didn't read the legal stuff. And I bonded with it. Though I'd always loved John Donne and George Herbert and Hopkins, when I read through Genesis, I felt, "Oh, this is mine. It's *mine*. These men and women are my mother and father." That embrace was immediate—like being metal pulled into a magnet.

JL: Tribal identification?

AO: I can't even say, except the word "mine." *It's mine.* These are my stories, these men and women are my mothers and fathers, this God is my God whether I like Him or not; sometimes I do and sometimes I don't. But to say "heritage" makes it sound distant. It didn't feel distant, but felt as if this was already part of me, an integral part of which I had been unconscious.

JL: Did your family ever acknowledge any of the holy days?

AO: We didn't do any of that, and I had no expectation of what I would experience. I identified with the rebels, I identified with Sarah laughing. I identified with Jacob wrestling. And I loved how when Jacob wrestles with the unknown Being until dawn—the unknown assailant is called "a man," but we're supposed to know that it's an angel or something on that order, or God—the man says, "Let me go, for day is coming." And Jacob says, "I will not let thee go, except thou bless me." I can hardly say that line now without bursting into tears: "I will not let thee go, except thou bless me."

JL: Irresistible language.

AO: The idea of "I won't let go until you give me a blessing" is so powerful and moving to me. And I didn't do anything with it for decades. I did do one thing: if you walk into my house you'll see an etching I made in graduate school (I used to do a lot of graphic art)—imitation Matisse in his linear style—of Jacob wrestling the angel. They're both horizontal, and Jacob is gritting his teeth and looking strained, and the angel is smiling because the angel *wants* Jacob to ask for that blessing.

JL: This story helps me appreciate the intimacy of your relationship with the Bible—this hasn't been primarily an intellectual exercise for you.

AO: It becomes intellectual, it becomes everything. But it's physical, it's emotional, it's intellectual, it's the works. And it's nothing that I was raised to do.

JL: What were you raised to do?

AO: I was raised to be a good Jew, which in my parents' and grandparents' view meant to be an A student, and be kind, and struggle against prejudice and for peace—all good lefty things. Be a good lefty Jew.

JL: When you were a college student making the discovery that this was yours, you had already engaged deeply with poetry. Did you know at that point that you were a writer?

AO: I wrote all the time. My mother was an English major, and she wrote poetry; she read poetry to me from the time I had ears. Shakespeare and Tennyson and Browning.

JL: So as a very small child, you were hearing poetry.

AO: I was hearing poetry and I wrote poetry, but I never thought of myself as a poet. I didn't think of myself as a quote-unquote "poet" until I had been a college teacher for many years and was asked what my identity was at a writer's and artist's colony. For many years my identity was student, then wife and mother, then English teacher—and I also wrote poetry.

JL: But it was "also."

AO: It was "also." I wouldn't have gotten my job at Rutgers, I think, if they had known I did that. I can say that now.

JL: I see that you have a copy of *the volcano sequence*. My experience reading it connects with what you're been saying about the Torah, and about the young poem-writing you. *the volcano sequence* begins with the masculine pronoun for God (you say in one poem, "God who disguises Himself as world") and moves gradually into the indwelling female energy that you end with. And of course some of these poems are addressed to "the speaker's" (as we've been taught to say) mother.

[*AO laughs*]

JL: I'm glad to hear you laugh. Okay, I'm going to say it: *your* mother.

AO: Let's say it: my mother. Or Mother, because my experience in writing was that I was channeling the voice. The voice was speaking sometimes to God and sometimes to my mother, but my quote-unquote "mother" was also capital-M "Mother": partly mine, partly anybody's, partly the archetype.

JL: One poem says, "Whoever is speaking in these pages, I welcome you. Let me be your vehicle." Did you literally feel as if you were channeling the poems?

AO: Yes, in this book. The backstory of this book is that I'd had a poetry block for three years. Not fun.

JL: Horrible.

AO: Yes, horrible. I could write essays, I could write book reviews, I could write anything that required me only from the neck up. I was out of touch, I didn't have access to my heart or my soul. Any poetry I wrote was junk, and I was desperate.

I was in therapy, and one day I was looking at this guidebook to the island of Thera, which in Greek mythology was a volcanic island that, when it erupted, produced a tsunami that drowned Atlantis. Big Greek myth! I was looking at a beautiful photograph of white volcanic crust, and it started speaking; but it was its voice and my voice at the same time. It started speaking about the history of destructive anger that was mine and my mother's, and what it's like to be an extinct volcano that destroyed the place of the golden age.

I'd known that if you're blocked it's because there's something under the rock that you don't want to think about. How do you think about it if you can't think about it! And these opening poems about destructive rage, which I recognized as *my* destructive rage, were telling me things about myself that I didn't want to know. But I immediately recognized it: *Oh, this is it!* So I made a literal, conscious deal with the poems: "If you agree to keep arriving, I agree not to tell you what to say." And did that for a year. They arrived intermittently, and I did feel as if I was channeling them. And they were saying things I couldn't have said if I hadn't made that deal.

JL: Thank you for letting me in on this—letting us in on it.

AO: The anger in the poems—the anger at God and the anger at my mother—was explosive. These were things that I would have kept under the surface.

JL: You not only let the poems in and wrote them down, you boldly published them. This groundbreaking book must have

liberated other people to deal with their anger at God and
their anger at their mothers and at themselves.

AO: I hope so. Writing it enabled me to work it through: at the
beginning it's all anger, and by the end of the book it's gotten
tender.

JL: Would you read "dark smile"?

AO: Yes—The book works its way toward the idea of the Shek-
hinah, the feminine aspect of God, who is also all our moth-
ers. To turn and face one's own biological mother and find the
divinity in her—it's tremendously hard. Impossible. [*reads:*]

DARK SMILE

Just now, coming downstairs after returning some books to a shelf
and reading a few pages of a friend's book, his piece on Jacob's
wrestling, I was flooded with love for this friend, and in my
happiness halfway down the stairs I thought to glance at my
interior—
there, very faintly, was the claw of the shekhinah,
probing; there too was her dark smile.

∿

when she comes it will not be from heaven, it will be up from the
    cunts and breasts

it will be from our insane sad fecund obscure mothers

it will be from our fat scrawny pious wild ancestresses their claws

their fur and their rags

(*the volcano sequence*)

JL: Thank you! It's a long leap from the beginning of the book.
One of your epigraphs quotes Buber's phrase "the eternal
Thou." I experience that phrase as masculine, but by the time
you reach this point in the book, it's not male anymore.
"Cunts and breasts," whoa! But I love the claw; it's not a pretty
thing; it's a hard thing.

AO: The women's spirituality movement wants the goddess to be
nice. Well, she's not nice.

JL: She's also Kali, the destroyer of unreality.

AO: Yeah.

JL: I've always disliked the word "goddess." Like "poetess," it feels like a diminutive; but we had to embrace it in the '70s.

AO: Well I still go for it. I like "goddess"; it feels big to me and not necessarily pretty. It feels like energy to me.

JL: Can you talk about how you got from "This is mine"—your college experience of reading the Bible—to really making it yours, making it female?

AO: I didn't do much with it, except for that one etching, until the mid-'80s. Then, pretty much out of the blue, came this episode of thinking about the book of Job and Job's wife. That came right after finishing *Stealing the Language* and writing about women poets rewriting mythology.

The mythology I was looking at was classical myths and fairytales; that book was in press. And one night I found myself thinking about the book of Job and the double ending, where Job says he's sorry he said anything, and then God rewards him. In what's supposed to be a happy ending, he gets his health back and his wealth back—and suddenly I thought about Job's wife. How did she feel about this happy ending where she gets ten new children to replace the ten that God let Satan kill off at the beginning of the story? I thought "Whoa! Hold on there!" and madly started writing from the point of view of Job's wife, asking what *she* would have to say when she got up the courage to challenge God the way her husband had. And when I saw what I'd written, I knew I was on that train you can't get off: I will be—this will be my wrestling.

JL: Was this the beginning of your work with Midrash?

AO: Yes. What came out of that experience was the book *The Nakedness of the Fathers: Biblical Visions and Revisions*, part retelling biblical stories, part autobiography, part prose and part poetry. I didn't know what I was doing except that I was compelled to do it, to read these stories and retell them, spin them my way. I hadn't even heard the word "midrash" before I started doing this. Once I found myself writing about the Bible, I had to study Hebrew. I'm not a scholar, and I thought, "What right do I have to do any of this?" I started reading a lot and learning a lot—and that's where I learned what Midrash was, what the Shekhinah was, and a lot else. That was a big learning curve. And then I did a lot of writing about the Bible.

JL: Your description of *The Nakedness of the Fathers* as part prose, part poetry, reminds me that I've heard you speak about language poetry—about being somewhat allergic to it. But it seems to me you've always been challenging poetic conventions, perhaps in way that that might anticipate or be willing to occupy the same bed that some of the language poets do. Much of what you've done is unconventional; you experiment with form, with stream of consciousness, you change gears from poetry to prose and back again.

AO: The difference is that I don't read a lot of language poetry, but it seems as if it's about breaking things down and finding less meaning, and what I'm interested in is finding more meaning. But I'm too ignorant about language poetry to say anything except that I find it hard to read.

JL: I have a hunch you'd really like Bernadette Mayer; I've been reading her lately, and I see some affinities. But that's another conversation.

AO: I do like to write outside the box.

JL: And from what you've said, I get the sense that something like channeling or receiving is a large part of what goes on in your process.

AO: I'm grateful when that happens.

JL: Do you ever try to force it?

AO: How can you?

JL: Some people try. For example, you had training in received forms and traditional metrics, so you could say to yourself, "Okay, I'm going to write a sonnet or a villanelle." But that doesn't seem to be your way of working.

AO: Well, I can write in traditional closed forms and so can you; I did it by ear, by instinct, when I was young. It was easy and fun. In a way, it is harder to write in open form. You don't know where you're going from moment to moment, and if you're writing iambic pentameter it's doing half the work for you. Once you've learned how to do that, you can just do it. But writing in open forms is like jazz improvisation. A line has to be related to the line before, but you can't tell exactly how until you do it, and then the one after that has to be related, and it all has to sound right. Whatever that is!

JL: When you broke into open forms were you reading other

convention-breakers? Ginsberg, the Beats? Who was on your mind?

AO: The first open-form poem I ever wrote was in graduate school. I had a couple of men friends—one was a novelist, one was a poet, and I was giving them lunch—and I thought they were my friends. I was writing exclusively in traditional forms at that time, I thought that was the right way, I thought real poetry was formal poetry. And they ganged up on me and said, "Why don't you write like a twentieth-century American?"

JL: What year was this?

AO: It would have been 1962 or '63.

JL: That was when everything was changing.

AO: I was furious at them, and I defended myself and formal poetry. Then they left, and I felt totally betrayed because they'd been so mean to me. Then I said to myself, "What they want is so easy—I can do that." So I sat down and I wrote my first open-form poem, and it was about my family—I had never written about my family before. It was about my mother and my father and my sister, and it was—oh! Breaking the form was liberating in a way I had not anticipated.

JL: That was the early '60s, when there was such a strong sense of "us and them." It was as if there was a war between the so-called academic poets and the Beats, the West Coast poets, the poets who were reading in coffee houses. "Howl" had been published in the '50s, but it was—

AO: Yes, but I hadn't read it, and I was still pretty prim and proper. I was still in graduate school, and getting an extremely traditional training. Only after I started teaching did I really began reading the poetry of my own time. I had to teach contemporary poetry, and it was one discovery after another. That's when I realized that I was not only a daughter of Whitman, but I was a daughter of William Carlos Williams and Allen Ginsberg.

JL: What about Muriel Rukeyser? Were you aware of her at that point?

AO: I was dimly aware of Rukeyser but—this is another strange thing—I wasn't reading her until much later—until I had a graduate student, Anne Herzog, who wanted to write her dissertation on Rukeyser.

So then I had to read Rukeyser, and that was a revelation.

But the first Rukeyser poem I remember reading in some anthology and being impressed by was "Effort at Speech Between Two People." I was a child, a preteen; I remember the room in which I read it, and I moved from that room when I was ten or eleven. On the one hand I didn't understand it, and on the other hand I understood it perfectly: "This is about my mother and father and everyone. It's about me; it's about everyone not being able to talk to each other." And it sank in.

JL: I wonder if the form of that poem on the page sank in as well; it's a poem where she uses colons floating in lots of space.

AO: Right. It didn't look like any poem I had ever read. And it didn't sound like any poem, and it wasn't sentences, it was fragments.

JL: So at ten did some part of you know, "This is mine"?

AO: It was mine, it became mine, but I don't think any part of me consciously knew that.

JL: The time you're talking about was just before the explosion of women writing poems about women, for women, to women—when the books by Judy Grahn and Adrienne Rich and Audre Lorde burst on our consciousness.

AO: Which I only caught up with in the '70s when I'd been editing Blake's complete poetry for Penguin. It was 200 pages of notes—I was completely absorbed in William Blake—and when I picked my head up and breathed air, there was the women's poetry movement going on all around us. I had a lot of catching up to do. It was thrilling! And it was painful, so much of it was like a knife in one's heart—feeling what it was one was living through.

JL: Can you say more? Was the knife an awareness of all of the losses that. . . .

AO: Well, of history of course, but also I was the first woman in my department, and it was a very highly esteemed department in which women were not esteemed.

JL: You were the first woman faculty member in your department?

AO: At Rutgers University.

JL: My god!

AO: Which was a boys' school when I started teaching there. It went coed only with great reluctance from the Rutgers faculty. Though I also got to teach at Douglass College—all women. It was ironic: Rutgers looked down at Douglass, but when I was teaching at Douglass the women were brighter, worked harder, were altogether better as students than the men. So it went. But the sense of living in a world where the dice were stacked against me hurt so much when I became aware of it.

JL: Can you talk about the relationship between your life as a teacher and your writing life, especially your poem-writing life?

AO: One of the things that happened after I finished with Blake was I didn't want to teach Blake anymore; I wanted to teach women's poetry. Luckily, my department was so large that I could go to my chair and say, "I don't want to teach romantic poetry anymore. I don't want to teach Blake. I want to teach a course in women's poetry." And they could say "okay." And later, when I said, "I want to teach a course called The Bible and Feminist Imagination," they could say, "What do you want to do that for?" But they let me do it.

JL: It sounds as if the courses you taught have fed your imagination—

AO: Totally—yes. I was fortunate to be at Rutgers, because it was such a huge department that I could drop this and pick up that; someone else could teach romantic poetry, and it didn't matter; I was able to teach anything I wanted to. If I'd been in a smaller place, I'd have been stuck in the same slot year after year. For that, I'm really grateful to Rutgers—although I was quite angry at Princeton for not giving me a job.

JL: Was that when Jerry began teaching there?

AO: Jerry and I were applying for jobs all over the country. We were both new PhDs; we both thought we were a good bet. I had a book in press, my dissertation was coming out, and this was at a time when people who hadn't finished their dissertations were getting jobs. So we both applied to Princeton. Guess what?

JL: He got a job.

AO: He got a job, and I got a letter saying, "Dear Miss Ostriker." Not "Dr." And you know when someone addresses you in a letter as "Miss," you might as well tear that letter up and not bother to read it. It was a very short letter; it burned itself instantly into my brain: "Dear Miss Ostriker, As a glance at our catalog might have informed you, our faculty here at

Princeton is entirely male. Therefore my reply to your query must be in the negative. Very truly yours, signed, the Chairman." And that was legal then.

JL: Those were the days.

AO: The year was 1964.

JL: Oof.

AO: It was legal.

JL: You've had to shed a few lives and a few skins to get here; and you've had to challenge a lot and sometimes accept the unacceptable.

AO: If I'd gotten the job at Princeton that I wanted to get, it would have been wonderful in some ways, but I would have taught nothing but romantic poetry.

JL: The eternal Thou had another plan for you, perhaps!

I'd like to ask about what has changed in your writing. I don't know how you've experienced your evolution as a poet and how you'd characterize it, but it seems to me that in your recent book, *The Old Woman, the Tulip, and the Dog*—but even before that—the poems are more condensed and immediate, more playful, and even more hopeful. Something in the "argument" feels different. Each of the three speakers has something to say in each poem, but it's always the dog—the earthy, bawdy dog—who gets the last word. This book has a different quality, as I read it, from the sense of wrestling with the angel of earlier work. I'm wondering if you see it that way, if you feel more hopeful.

AO: I do, and it does seem as if there's less pain, less struggle, less anger in myself and in my writing than there was. I don't feel as if I'm always battling something. Wrestling is good, but there are other things one can do. For years—for decades—I remember a younger self, myself, that would pray, "Please, God,"—the God I don't believe in—"can you please give me some serenity, have me not always struggling?" And that has sorta kinda come to pass. I'm still a worrying, anxious, often angry creature, but there are great, long stretches of serenity.

JL: One way you seem to work that out in your poetry is in your empathy with artists. In a poem from *The Book of Seventy*, you look at three painters who made art into their old age, and I can see the visual artist in you. I'd love to hear you read the section of "Ars Poetica: Three Poems" that begins "Matisse, too."

AO [*reads*]:

Matisse, too, when the fingers ceased to work
worked larger and bolder, his primary colors celebrating
the weddings of innocence and glory, innocence and glory

Monet when the cataracts blanketed his eyes
painted swirls of rage, and when his sight recovered
painted water lilies, Picasso claimed

I do not seek, I find, and stuck to that story
about himself, and made that story stick.
Damn right. We are talking about defiance.

(The Book of Seventy)

JL: Defiant to the end—and you also embrace these artists' sen-
suousness, largeness of vision, and—may I say hopefulness?

AO: Something like that; I think it happens to people over sixty.
And the culture doesn't makes it any easier; there's no real
respect for people over sixty, any more than there's real respect
in the culture for mothers. But something clicks and you be-
come more at ease with your life.

JL: What you're saying brings to mind your poem "To a Preg-
nant Woman"—it's so earthy and gorgeous. Will you read it?

AO [*reads*]:

TO A PREGNANT WOMAN

Years ago the bigger girls used to whisper
and laugh, excluding you
their bags crammed with lipsticks and cigarettes
their full sweaters facing the other way
it hurt you not to hear
what they were saying
soon you will learn a secret said the old woman
larger than any bag can hold, an old
riotous tale of seduction and addiction
—motherhood! you yourself are going to whisper and laugh

Soon your waters will break said the dark red tulip
you will turn inside out
much as my bulb split open

in order to deliver me
up through packed dirt into fresh air and much as I
will ultimately reveal my inner secrets
by dying
plenty of pain for us all
but my dear you
are going to produce your own interior sweet bulb

Get ready said the dog
for smells different from any you have known
mysterious infant scalp smell belly smell
creamy shit smell dried milk smell
foot smell
the odors of your own body
will be different more fruity more ripe
your hands never have felt
anything delectable as a baby's skin
enjoy the trance while it lasts

(The Old Woman, the Tulip, and the Dog)

JL: Ah, it's a trance, isn't it?

AO: It is a trance.

JL: And smell is to be enjoyed. You are, in your poems and in your life, an enjoyer of everything there is.

AO: I would like to be more in my life an enjoyer of everything that is. But I think a key line here is also when the tulip says, kind of casually, "plenty of pain for us all."

JL: But without a narrative of all the different kinds of pain— personal pain and the pain of the world.

AO: Right. Just as I think the tulip is practically Buddhist at that moment.

JL: You talk about suffering as necessary for freedom in one of your earlier poems, and there's an echo of it in *the volcano sequence* where you say "O to grow means pain." But here, pain is accepted and you don't dwell on it. Yet for me one of the most memorable moments in all your writing is in *The Mother/Child Papers*, in a prose section where you write about the experience of that damn doctor giving you a spinal block against your wishes. It brings up the rage I feel at all that arrogance.

AO: Yeah.

JL: —and control! It persists in so many places.

AO: Like practically everywhere.

JL: Practically everywhere. And yet, when you address the Shekhinah in these poems, I do hear a kind of hope. I'd love to hear you read "Bright Star and Devil Moon."

AO [*reads*]:

Let there be a return of the repressed
let the women be fountains of light and energy
flooding the world hallelujah said the old woman

Let me exfoliate fiercely let me and mine
increase and multiply said the dark red tulip
becoming more magnificent each generation

Let me be the one who represents faith
said the dog
now you see anything can happen

> (*The Old Woman, the Tulip, and the Dog*)

JL: That would be a perfect place to end this conversation, except that I have one more question for you. It's this: after all your many interviews, is there a still a question you wish someone would ask?

AO: Well, I always tell my students: kill the censor, write what you're afraid to write. And you could ask me, "What are you afraid to write?" And my answer would be, "I won't tell you."

JL: Nothing to say on what you've most feared, what you've most needed courage for?

AO: I can't tell you what I'm still afraid to write because I'm still afraid to talk about it.

JL: I can't wait for the next channeled book! Alicia, thank you so much—this has been an illumination.

AO: Thank you, Joan.

JENNY FACTOR

Alicia Ostriker, World-Builder
The Imaginary Lover, Green Age, *and Other*
Points of Fusion with William Blake

> *Earnestly, they sit in my office*
> *Showing me their stigmata . . .*
> *And I sympathize. Then they try on their ambitions*
> *Like stiff new hiking boots, and I laugh*
> *And approve, telling them where to climb.*
> FROM "LISTEN" IN THE IMAGINARY LOVER

William Blake was born in 1757. Before he was a poet, he was an original—an engraver-artist-craftsman, and a friend to radical thinkers of his day. He was an iconoclast. Alicia Suskin Ostriker was born in 1937. Painting and the visual arts were her first, primary loves. As an undergraduate and graduate student, Ostriker discovered Blake's life and poetry, and his work left an enduring imprint on her creative sense of self. Ostriker too developed an interest in radical movements—especially antiwar and women's movements. Ostriker's first sound-driven book of poetry was called simply *Songs* (1969), perhaps echoing Blake's own early books, *Songs of Innocence and of Experience.*

This is an essay about mentorship: the warm, interpersonal mentorship Ostriker describes in "Listen," above, and the silent internalized mentorship that her favorite books provided to her when she was a beginning author—those that, while written by others even long dead, serve as a kind of compass to her personal geography.

Ostriker is a bold, innovative scholar and poet who has spent her half century in academia devoted to three primary projects. Her critical feminist consideration of a new women's poetry, which began in essays in the early 1980s, culminated in her break-out work, *Stealing the Language: The Emergence of Women's Poetry in America* (1986). Later her feminist reinterpretation of the Old Testament resulted in several books on spiritual themes, most notably *The Nakedness of the Fathers: Biblical Visions and Revisions* (1994). These two critical projects—both feminist—make obvious sense for readers of Ostriker's creative oeuvre: each of her early poetry books speaks with a strong woman's voice, nodding to some of the critical observations of *Stealing the Language*, including image-references to the crass and sublime functions of the body, use of humor, and use of curse. A harder argument, however, would need to be made to link Ostriker's creative output to her very first important academic project—definitive editorial and scholarly consideration of the work of William Blake. In 1965, Ostriker published her graduate thesis on Blake, *Vision and Verse in William Blake*; in 1977, she served as editor to Penguin's *William Blake: The Complete Poems*. This third project on Blake can be harder to understand as a critical *and* creative enterprise.

Nevertheless, in "The Road of Excess: My William Blake" (1990), Ostriker assesses the influence of her Blake scholarship on her work as a contemporary *woman* poet. Ostriker compares her project to Blake's in three ways: the refusal of the inner censor, the use of humor to diffuse cosmic tensions, and the use of personal extrapoetic visionary experience to anchor her most radical poems. Citing Blake's "For everything that lives is holy, life delights in life," she writes, "He articulated for me a sense of reality which had been inarticulately mine since childhood" (69). She continues:

> Blake to me has been hero, lover, and ally, has been standard bearer and courage bearer, has been the chosen teacher to whom I attributed all wisdom, has been an antagonist in that mental fight in which opposition is true friendship, and has latterly become the paternal figure from which I most gratefully deviate. (68)

Ostriker's essay on Blake is a wonderful example of how scholarly acts can become creative, even intimate, and about the way that reading and writing are transmaterial, transpersonal, and even intergenerational. Ostriker reconsiders gender issues in Blake's poetry while teaching his work to her then-current group of students. While "it seemed [Blake] knew whatever there was to know about destroying tyranny within the self and within society," he is "miraculously able to perceive Man as infinite, [but] he cannot perceive women so" (73). As she continues thinking aloud with her students, Ostriker describes Blake at once as "the first man I ever read who seemed to know that sex was about love, not war, breathtaking equality rather than conquest," and yet for whom while Nature was "female, female was Nature, to be born was to be maternally entrapped and even crucified by her" (75).

Ostriker remarks in particular on the ways in which Blake's virtuous women either behave as passive victims or are portrayed as succubae and aggressors, especially in their roles as mothers. In doing so, she is separating out her creative self from his. If Blake's women are victims or villains, certainly, palpably, her own are not. Rather, Ostriker's women are speakers and subjects, complex subject-actors, larger-than-life ambivalent progenitors of the stories and life histories that comprise her poems. While Blake's poetry is not peopled by actual children, Ostriker's sometimes is. Blake hardly ever uses the personal subjective narrative—*my* child, *my* wife, *my* home, *my* story; his project is closer to world building—*this is* childhood, *this is* experience, *this is* democracy, *this is* the origin of God. By contrast, Ostriker frequently speaks from the perspective of the first person singular. Her poems in all the books leading up to the production of her Blake essay are peopled with her subjective and specific others—two daughters, one scientific and one more creative, a son, a husband who is a scientist-scholar, students, a mother, a father, friends. Any broader perspective on the world that she provides at that point is implied in the poem's backdrop, or attributed directly and subjectively to the ideas and thoughts of the poem's speaker.[1]

One commonality, however, is that in relation to poets of their day, Blake and Ostriker seem to share the same sound-related project or critique: although both have good ears for language, neither lets pure "ear" drive the poem forward or determine its decision-making trajectory. Message, mode, and intention are more important to each of these poets. In fact, one might argue that craft-and-deviation *is* ideology in Blake, never versifying as its own destination.

Like Ostriker, Blake began as a craftsman—not just an engraver-apprentice but also a formal versifier. Although his later works in epic (projects completed between 1804 and 1820) deviate from traditional meter and rhyme, his early work and shorter lyrics are tightly crafted, especially in *Songs of Innocence*, and its apposite companion, *Songs of Experience*. Ostriker is closest to a versifying project in *Songs*, but after that very seldom returns to more formal elements of verse form, preferring the syntactic prosody of the discursive Biblical line—though that too might be construed as a gesture of "excess." Ostriker describes Blake's craft this way: "Pursuing the road of excess and unorthodoxy in his prosody as in his ideology,

Blake began by writing the lyric poems for which he is still best known, in lines that sounded like nursery rhymes because he was attempting to produce or reproduce within the reader *certain kinds of pure and primitive experiences"* (emphasis mine) (69–71). When framing Blake's prosody as a gesture toward the primitive corporeal, the expansive, and often allegorical place where the personal and political meet, Ostriker might be describing her own poetry as well.

Blake's influence on Alicia Ostriker seems to center on three areas of shared project:

(1) Devotion to psychic repair, to marriage as metaphor for the resolution of split frames of mind and reference

(2) Issues of scale that mark a tendency to hold self and others of equal size and complexity within each poem's frame

(3) A search for a vantage point on the personal and political, specifically seeking the imagined vantage point of God

The themes driving two books of Ostriker's written in midlife, *Green Age* (1989) and *The Imaginary Lover* (1986), are the maternal erotic, especially the love of the mother for her growing and separating children; heterosexual love as seen in the marriage of equals; and the love of the adult woman for her own life. Along the way, the woman adjusts how she carries her burdens. The woman's life carries the repercussions of sexual and political violence, and the marriage carries a lot of personal and sociopolitical history, including her feminism, her work, and her rape. The woman is herself an adult daughter engaging in acts of repair with her past, especially with her own mother. The woman as artist also engages in acts of repair—with historical women artists, with women artists who are her friends, with students, and with the reader. Throughout these two books, the speaker's voice embraces and owns its contradictions and opinions.

To See the World in a Grain of Sand

One of the most fruitful tensions in William Blake's poetry is in his devotion to psychic repair, to literal and nonliteral "marriage" as a metaphor for the resolution of split frames of mind and reference. Ostriker describes Blake as splitting the earth's original whole into "gendered fragments." His "recurring themes struggle between Reason and Energy or repressive reason and passionate energy"

(79–81). When two energies are equal and in balance, this is good. Repression of any one energy, for Blake, creates a kind of imbalance that to him is tantamount to evil. As Blake metaphorically declares here and in a hundred other places, "A Robin Redbreast in a Cage / puts all Heaven in a Rage."

The creation of apposites is a generative impulse vital to both Blake and Ostriker. Blake enacts this clearly in *Songs of Innocence and of Experience* and again in "The Marriage of Heaven and Hell." Paradoxical yankings of opposites are repeated *microscopically* in phrases such as these from "Auguries of Innocence"—"To see the World in a Grain of Sand / And a Heaven in a Wild Flower, / Hold Infinity in the palm of your hand")—and more *macroscopically* throughout the allegories of the more "prophetic" poems. Showing a distinction between similarities, Blake holds the ugly and beautiful side by side in the Tyger's "fearful symmetry." Showing a similarity inside a difference, he responds with "The Question Answered." Here, what men "do require" and what women "do require" leads to the same refrain: "The lineaments of Gratified Desire." Men and woman, far from dissimilar, need from love the selfsame thing.

The fruitful resolution of opposites, an espousal of double-valence, is almost a Blakean philosophy—a way of seeing the true nature of the world, the trend toward which all elementals deserve a push centerward. Marsha Keith Schuchard compares Blake to Yeats in *Why Mrs. Blake Cried: William Blake and the Sexual Basis of Spiritual Vision*, calling his method of double-valence along the truth of the body, a "sexual spiritual philosophy" (10).

If marriage is abstruse philosophy in Blake, it is literal and personal in the middle works of Ostriker. The opening of "Words for a Wedding" from *Green Age*—whose title implies a personal valediction and ongoing relationship between poet and listener—is "Free and rejoicing, walk into this prison." The line itself, with its axiomatic sense of truth and paradox, could be mistaken for one of Blake's. How she builds out the metaphor, though, while Blakean in how the poem provokes our squirming anticipation of how energy will respond to repression, is in impact and gendered conflict resolution, very true to Ostriker's own playful and colorful imagistic sense.

A door is clanging loudly, . . .
. . . notic[e] the stains,
Scrawls, chips in the wall, stink,

The will of those before you to escape.

Yet, unlike Blake's marital protagonists, these lovers have a shared secret: "Now feel in your pocket for the scrap / Of mirror the guards forgot. . . ." Ostriker's protagonists have hope, not that together they may be able to remake the world's repressions, but that they can subvert and endure them.

In Blake's "I saw a chapel all of gold," instead of a jagged piece of mirror, a weaponized vehicle of freedom, an exterior entrant, a serpent, intrudes to repress and defile true love.

> . . . I saw a serpent rise between
> The white pillars of the door
> And he forcd & forcd & forcd. . . .

> . . . Vomiting his poison out
> On the bread & on the wine. . . .

Allegories both of true pure love and dangerous convention-based counterventions, these poems by Ostriker and Blake are in a sense one another's apposite. The poems are similarly shaped: Ostriker's fifteen short lines resemble Blake's sixteen. By contrast, the place of perfect love and beauty in Blake is one where "the people" weep outside. A different phallic symbol—not mirror shard but serpent— serves as interlocutor, penetrating its unsulliable depths. The symbol of the snake, considered by some scholars as "repression" (Leopold Damrosch 204–14), comes to defile the temple where otherwise lovers could be *true* lovers. The rising serpent's actions that force, force, force also look like rape, which becomes a theme in Ostriker's later work. Ostriker's view of marriage in this poem is the warmer and more hopeful one; protagonists enter a prison that is the social stricture, marriage, but love and the true reflection of the authenticity of the other serve as mirror, knife, force of escape, allowing the lovers a breathing space inside paradox.

For Blake, the benedictions and benefits of love itself are inevitably punctured; the prisons are not merely walls, the serpent itself is part of the story—Eden's rightful end. And yet how alike are these poems in their elemental parts, which embed marriage and love with convention, repression, and paradox, not as two enemies that can be separated, but as inevitable bedfellows. Ostriker's mirror perhaps shares something with the mirror of Old Testament midrash, invoked and interpreted by Avivah Zornberg in *The Particulars of Rapture*. For Zornberg, the wives of Israel helped their enslaved husbands in Egypt see themselves as nonslaves on their one date night weekly in the fields, by hiding a mirror fragment in a basket with their bread (57–63). In the Biblical echo, Ostriker taps into a deep root of metaphysics found in Blake.

Ostriker depicts marriage as a struggle of powerful and equal forces in "In the Twenty-Fifth Year of Marriage, It Goes On" from *The Imaginary Lover*, as a speaker argues against entrapment, inauthenticity, and frustration:

> Damn it, honey, neither one of us
> Is the victim of the other one, how
> About admitting that for starters?

The gritty strength of "In the Twenty-Fifth Year of Marriage" comes from what the poem is willing to cop to—two figures behaving badly but enduring in the end. In the second section, the speaker wonders aloud whether her husband, who was not home when the brutal attack occurred, blames himself for her rape ten years prior, and uses the poem as a place to remind him that she saved herself in the decade that followed, and that she thinks this is as it should be. She saved her life by staying alive then, and later saved her spirit from the toilet bowl of shame threatening to flush her. Thirty years later, Ostriker writes in "Anger II: The Rape" that "one feels covered in slime and shit" (*The Old Woman, the Tulip, and the Dog*). She clearly feels this work was *hers* to do, and preferable to him wearing the mask of Man with her in order to "save" her.

The depiction of issues of gender and power in this marriage is everything feminists might hope for in Blake but do not get. The wife "In the Twenty-Fifth Year of Marriage" wants to be seen as surviving, wants to be valued and allowed her rich, complex self, and all her alternate selves, even when they are shrewish, motherish, desiring. She wants to free herself of her "Jewish mama tragedy mask"; she wants her husband also to free himself of entanglement, eschew wearing the mask of Man, that of "clever / White man scientist." Both members of the couple have power, in their own lives and vis-à-vis one another, however misused it is at times—within the poem, the husband threatens to jump out the window, the wife "laughing / Her horse teeth sticking out" says "Why don't / You . . . ?" In the end, the two resolve their conflict not by ending but by shocking, laughing, de-escalating, and continuing in paradox.

"Whom would I wrestle with if not with you. / Don't throw me out any / More windows, you say. . . ." The poem concludes:

> We seem to be joking and
> Making love, we seem
> Peculiarly mirthful together, as if
> We had a tiny secret, like children
> . . . as if
> It doesn't matter how mad
> We are . . .
> . . . we are in this marriage for life,
> Life that is always surprising us,
> As my father used to say,
> With some kind of kick in the tail.

In that final statement Ostriker's and Blake's paradoxes of marriage brush elbows. Marriage may be full of contradiction, but vital, centering, and numinous along its round, world-growing edge.

Though Blake and Ostriker each place marriage in an enclosed space at times, noting the overlay of repression in marital erotic love, Ostriker is quite insistent to write in windows: "The mind and body satisfy / Like windows and furniture in a house" ("Wanting All"). Damrosch explores marriage in Blake as a particularly fruitful tension. He notes that Blake "turned psychosexual experience into [a varying and sometimes heterogeneous] philosophical structure" (211), a gesture Ostriker uses often as well. For Ostriker, the push and pull of human relation becomes the currency of philosophy.

My Mother Groaned, My Father Wept, into the Dangerous World I Leapt

When the close relationship described by Ostriker's speaker is one of marriage's surrogates—motherhood, daughterhood, friendship with a man—Ostriker's poems use a ramping-up of complexity, paradox, and problems of size to create a round and fleshed-out feminist world building. In the poems of motherhood that appear in *The Imaginary Lover* and *Green Age*, Ostriker applies marriage's nonresolution to the maternal erotic, electrifying the connection between mother and adult children. Fueled by the tension of *odi amo*, in this form of eros, the mother hates and loves, seeks to annihilate and to rebirth, to draw close and to allow space.

The theme of teen separation and angst emerges from the point of view of the mother. "This motherhood business fades, is almost over," she writes in "Mother in Airport Parking Lot." "And I remember everything. . . . between the / wailing birth cry // And the child's hand wave / . . . at the airport . . ." This poem's power is its portrayal of the mother staying behind "in love with asphalt . . . . Temporarily free and clear." The role of mother in the territory of self as a single, adult human, with her own choices to make, begins in a "parking lot," a place of liminal, temporary stasis, where objects of motion pause. The plane's "steel belly hurtles over me, // . . . pure sex." Phallic and female at once, the metallic, powerful airborne womb carries her child safe inside. The older woman simultaneously remembers every tender moment of motherhood and her own deep hope for herself and her ambitions for her future, savoring choices made and choices anticipated.

"Listen" and "A Question of Time" also trace this maternal erotic triangulation. Written as direct address—mother-speaker to individuating-daughter—the poems engage in emotional exchange fueling the drama underneath. "A Question of Time" opens:

I ask a friend. She informs me it is ten years
From when her mother wrote
"I hope at least you are sorry
For causing your father's heart attack,"
To now, when they are speaking
Weekly on the phone
And almost, even, waxing confidential.
I check my watch. Ten years is rather much,
But I am not a Texas fundamentalist,
And you are not a red-headed lesbian.
So it should take us shorter, . . .

This comparison of mother-daughter dyads is how Ostriker establishes that she and her daughter aren't speaking, just as her friend and her mother were not. What behaviors and what punishments, what sadisms and what countersadisms, child-to-mother and mother-to-child, have the right to lead to what lived outcomes? "I check my watch. Ten years is rather much," she continues. ". . . and I should get / Time off for good behavior / If I behave well, which / I do not plan to do." Instead, our speaker, knowing herself, plans to "pelt you with letters, gifts, advice . . . / . . . to beam a steady / Stream of anxiety / Rays which would stun a mule . . . / [as] . . .

you hack / Coldly away at this iron umbilicus, / Having sensibly put three thousand miles between us." The poem concludes:

> I remember you told me once, when we were still
> In love, the summer before you left
> For the hills of San Francisco, . . .
> To stop fearing estrangement:
> "Mom, you're not crazy like Grandma."
> It was the country. We were on the balcony . . .
> . . . I remember it was hot,
> How lightly we were dressed . . .
> And how you let me rest
> A half a minute in your suntanned arms.

On a balcony in nature, poised above and a little apart from life, the speaker's maternal romance is bathed in loss and warning. Motherhood's perfect moment is not enduring, is only a "half a minute." Her work as the mother to an infant is over, and her daughter is leaving her. But in this liminal space just past, all was as temporarily right as it was fleeting. The daughter's sweet nothing is not "I love you" but "You're not crazy like grandma." The moment of intimacy brings the mother just enough permission to spill out a small oil slick of possibly mis-sized and mistimed advice—"Don't do acid. It fries the brain." This mother is held, not big, but rather petite or equal-sized enough to fit in the daughter's lovely "suntanned arms."

The most powerful shift of person inside this poem involves not love or size but mirroring. Though called "A Question of Time," the poem really poses more a question of *identity* for the tough-minded mother-speaker. Are she and her daughter like the Texas Fundamentalist and red-headed Lesbian? No. Could she, as a mother (one notes ironically) "behave"? No. Is she like her own crazy mother? Yes. And her daughter's shifting identity seems to make her anxious: envisioned as the beautiful maiden, tan and relaxed, a wild young woman who may have become pregnant though her mother cautions her not to, a recreational drug user cautioned to avoid acid and cocaine, a poet whom the mother urges to keep up with her drawing and reading, a prisoner breaking free from babyhood into adulthood as she saws away at the "iron umbilicus." The broken mirror of "Words for a Wedding" is now appropriately the broken mirror of two women individuating.

One of the most challenging post-Freudian tensions the modern person navigates is to know, without distortion, what *size* we are inside our interactions, in the fluid spatial power dynamics within any dyad. Two women individuating while in dyad, and shifting across scale and size, is a process repeated in the poem "Listen." The mother, Ostriker herself, wants "to be a shrub," while her daughter wants to be a tree; mother hums "inaudibly" while wanting the daughter to "sing arias." The mother wants to lie down at the "foot of" the daughter's "mountain," and "rub the two dimes in my pocket / Together, while you dispense treasure / To the needy." This difference is of degree, magnitude and amplitude, rather than a difference of kind. The speaker describes a desired difference of *scale*—shrub/tree, poor/wealthy, needy/charitable, inarticulate/operatic—or a differentiating easier for the mother who feels abandoned to accept.

If Blake's cosmologic project imagined a "tyrannical rule by a God of Reason" and the various splittings of humanity and culture personified, then Ostriker persons this cosmology as her own in her earliest books. Her people are large. With Whitmanian mythic force, they contain multitudes. There is a tremendous sense of democracy in sizing others in this way. Whitman sized others this way. Adrienne Rich does too. But this kind of sizing in contemporary poetry is not the rule but the exception. Many poems traffic in a very natural contemporary mode of distortion. The self is of-size, many-dimensioned, forward and backward, broad (think Anne Sexton, think Ann Lauterbach, think Jorie Graham), or begins narrow and opens into a kind of broadness. The other is small, inert, inanimate, a kind of poem-furniture, until in the course of the poem the other gains dimension, grows, speaks until they become human in the speaker's/poet's consciousness and vantage point. Not for Ostriker. Her poems' people are human all along, human or magnificent, seeming larger than life—the daughter's dances are Dionysian, the husband is a circus performer. If there is a single element of worldview most unique to Ostriker's work, it is in this sizing, in the power, scale, potency, valence of self and other. In lines such as "The student poets visit, think me wise, / Think me generous . . . ," the speaker owns her own power. With clear-eyed perception, she accepts others—the students are pained and Christ-like with their "stigmata" or are brave with "ambitions / Like stiff new hiking boots," and as equals, "when they leave we hug." Every other in an Ostriker poem is an equal or similarly-able actor. There are no patsies.

Ostriker sizes others this way because she allows herself as a speaker to be spacious, to exist in complexity, including in terms of gender. Like Blake, whose gender Ostriker clearly experiences as broadened beyond male and female when he is most enlightened, Ostriker herself allows her identity as speaker to move into and out of gendered, genderless, and non-binary-gendered planes. "Meeting the Dead" features the genderqueer nature of Ostriker's othering. In a vision, Ostriker's speaker comes to peace with the ghost of her father. He inhabits her, in fact, as she drives along the freeway near Pasadena. In Ostriker's use of scaling and othering, gender demarcation does not hold.

Another important overlap between Blake's and Ostriker's voices appears in these poems' humor. Natural to Blake's populist voice, humor is also a vital tool. In Blake humor brings together the contradictory forces his poems seek to marry, such as "Prudence is a rich ugly old maid courted by Incapacity. . . . As the caterpillar chooses the fairest leaves to lay her eggs, so the priest lays his curse on the fairest joys. . . ." ("Proverbs of Hell," *The Marriage of Heaven and Hell*). According to Ostriker, "[Blake's] version of vision contains the dimension of humor. . . . I have the distinct sense that within the solemnity of all that is sacred is a grain of comedy. Dimly, it occurs to me that beyond my earshot, all around me, is laughter."

In Ostriker's "Listen," the speaker makes fun of herself while projecting all-sized imagery onto the Child-Other. The Child-Other is consort to gods whom the mother hopes will invite her to "teas and . . . dance recitals," is godlike herself dispensing charity, and is in the end small, a sea creature, trapped under her mother's hand. The mother-daughter dyad is unsettled and shifting. The mother can afford, in a sense, to empower her daughter through these images—making them bigger and smaller at will, bigger mostly because she feels less powerful in relation to her children now that they're grown. Yet she is also conscious that she is in the end the God of the poem, the creator both of the poem's life and her child's. Ostriker establishes this by depicting herself as mentor-god to the lives of her students, as if perhaps she can still convince her daughter of her value because other students see her that way. Even as Ostriker's speaker sizes her chosen objects all kinds of ways, she chuckles to herself. Humble, funny, a self-as-creator, Ostriker knows, with the surety of a God, that her young people, students as well as her own children, rely on her for their very primary ability to be at all, having given birth to them from her womb and from her pen. So if they are now wracked by Free Will and Wonder, if they separate and struggle, so be it. The language of love poetry characterizes the maternal erotics in both of these mother-daughter poems, making the Blakean marriage metaphor more than apt.

"Listen" begins with a mother telling her daughter about the students she counsels, who "think her wise" and who enjoy her and share time and intimacy with her.

> *Oh silly mother,* I can hear you mock.
> Listen, loveliest, I am not unaware
> This is as it must be.
> Do daughters mock their mothers? Is Paris
> A city? Do your pouring hormones
> Cause you to do the slam
> And other Dionysiac dances . . .

Reading this imagined dialogue, note the blend of love and humor, the distance between the parties—amicable but separate. With wry élan, the speaker answers a question with a question: "Do daughters mock their mothers? Is Paris / A city?" Answering a question with a question has a particularly winking, Jewish-mama tone.

Though the speaker in Ostriker's motherhood poems makes fun of herself, she is a formidable opponent—a lover of size whose desires take up space, not unlike the Jewish concept of a Jealous God. If Ostriker's poems resize in part because her ego is far from powerless, she doesn't imagine herself able to rewrite personal or social history and makes no attempt to resolve social and personal outrage morally or cleanly *ex machina* in these poems. Other poems throughout *Green Age* and *The Imaginary Lover*, such as "Stream," trace friendships with men that struggle with disequilibria of desire. "Hating the World" and "The Pure Products of America" recount friendships with women that crackle with different life views or with sensual intensities. When Ostriker's speaker portrays herself as a *daughter*, she and her mother find a way to connect through art as she declares "So my mother should have been a writer" and lays out her mother's life like a map she will be able to use to learn about herself—"Mother, chatterer, I ask you also, / You who poured Tennyson / And Browning into my child ear, and you / Who threw a boxful of papers, your novel / Down the incinerator / When you moved . . . / . . . Don't / Run away, tell me my duty, / I will try not to be deaf—" ("Surviving"). Ostriker's relational space where self meets others holds fast to Blake's best commitment to a "marriage ideal, as expressed especially in 'Jerusalem', [for a] mutually responsible and mutually loving covenant relationship," with room for separateness, a true "poetics of marriage" (George 127).

While her speaker and her others may move through many stories and sizes of self, and Ostriker may laugh at others and at herself, she does so seeking distance, optimal vantage point, and perspective. In all humility, she seeks grace, a neutral position of interpersonal harmony and understanding, an imaginary vantage point of God.

The Imaginary Vantage Point of God

So what does Ostriker's dialogue with Blake tell us about the poems? In *Dangerous Enthusiasm: William Blake and the Culture of Radicalism in the 1790s,* Jon Mee describes Blake as a "bricoleur," who in the Levi-Straussian sense uses the material at hand, rather than planning like an engineer. Not so much a world-builder as a cobbler of diverse substances (3), Blake said of himself, "I must create a system or be enslaved by another man's." Indeed, in his synesthesia of different modes of discourse, of primitivism, Bible, and historiography, Blake the Hebrew prophet is also Blake the Celtic bard. For both Blake and Ostriker, poetry is the vehicle and the method for cobbling an understanding of the world.

In the seven-part "Homage to Rumi" (*Green Age*), Ostriker wrestles with the very idea of God. Like Blake, Ostriker savors the spirituality of the body rather than the spirituality of traditional religion. In "A Meditation in Seven Days," she asks:

If a woman is a Jew
Of what is she the vessel

If she is unclean in her sex . . .

. . . a succubus, a flying vagina . . .

Succubus resonates with Blake as she speaks up for the body as a kind of holy ruler or instrument of measurement. As her own feminist self, she speaks up for the body of the woman as holy. As Eliot said of Blake, "We have the same respect for Blake's philosophies . . . that we have for an ingenious piece of home-made furniture; we admire the man who has put it together out of the odds and ends of the house" (Mee 9). In "Everywoman Her Own Theology" (*The Imaginary*

Lover), Ostriker cobbles a kitchen into a woman's holy space, and pins principles to her own church door, the refrigerator. "Out of the odds and ends of the house" Ostriker too is working!

Lately I've been spending afternoons reading poetry at the bedside of a very fine poet and Shoah survivor, Zahava Sweet. Zahava is eighty-four years old. Her eyesight, her hands, and her breath are failing her. But she knows language. And she knows metaphor. Her favorite book of poetry by far these days is Alicia Ostriker's *The Old Woman, the Tulip, and the Dog*. She asks me to read from it, and we meander our way through in no particular order—generally I read her a poem or two at a time.

And because it's hard to think clearly enough to *choose* a poem quickly and with intention in the institution's all-day dusk, I end up in a series of suspenseful accidents. Over and over again, I am surprised to find myself voicing my way through unexpected lines, trampling in poems that ricochet with resonance, catching both of us in the chest.

One day when Zahava was especially disoriented and bare, I read her, not knowing what I'd be reading, a poem from the book called, "The Beginning of Time": "They say it began and that it will end," I read, "the train in my dream flew above the earth . . .":

> . . . I see we are speedily approaching a tunnel
> in a forest hillside a rectangular entrance
> but unlike other tunnels this one is not black
> heavens inside the rectangle it is pure light
> . . . it will blind us and that will be the end of time
> the end of time and the beginning of God
> said the old woman

"The beginning of God," Zahava repeated in agreement. Then the tulip answers:

> My dear it is all in your mind that bed of confusion

She nodded . . .

> there is neither a beginning nor an end only a wheel trust me
> . . . then there are terrifying dreams
> mud is thrown at me I am trampled
> I am ripped apart I am burned alive
> I become ash, ash

Zahava drew in her breath sharply.

a shrieking wind destroys me in my dreams

She looked at me, and nodded with her eyes full. By the time we passed through the tulip and spoke the words of the dog, sleeping on the couch, trying to stay as near as possible to his owners' smell, we were both a little stunned. The mind of *this* poet seemed to have kept vigil with her, to have channeled Zahava's sleeplessness. Treblinka gaped clearly through the tulip's line breaks, and the minds of both women (the one in front of me and the maker of the poem) had matching chaos and hope and endings and light.

Reading into the timelessness of Alicia Ostriker's poetry, we were real and unreal at once, sitting near one another where a poem's light illuminated us to one another for an instant, more like lightning flash than fireglow. The poem tumbled along where my own empathic listening could not. The clock kept ticking on the wall above us, counting a time from a different dimension—the hour and minute hands quite literally mis-set and battery-lagging—counting a fictive nothing. The food tray sat at the foot of the bed as always, untouched and unappealing. I wondered where we were and when. Like Zahava, the poem's three figures are waiting on the human side of death's mystery. I wasn't sure how to turn the page.

This kind of dialogue, this wandering around inside a problem, wondering aloud inside a thinking, labeled in such a way that it becomes an embodied idea—it's one thing that poetic allegory does when it's done well. When it's done well is the caveat here. While allegory was one of the great poetic tools of the sixteenth, seventeenth, eighteenth, nineteenth, and even early twentieth (Great War era) centuries, not many poets writing today use allegory at all, let alone for the length of a slim but important book.

Reading these poems slowly, I find myself thinking hard about Alicia Ostriker's little dialogues (or tri-ologues) in *The Old Woman, the Tulip, and the Dog*, and how these poems function as vision or *allegory*, just as many of William Blake's did. The connections between Ostriker and Blake, scholar and subject, student and mentor, craftsperson and craftsperson, poet and poet, are profound. The generations *behind* Ostriker's poems open her work to reading that is also generational: Blake to Ostriker, Ostriker to Sweet, Sweet to me.

Note

1. I note, though, that in her books since roughly *the volcano sequence* (2002), the subjective other begins to go missing for an even more Blakean voice and mode, focusing even more directly on epic, philosophy, politics, and allegory.

Works Cited

Ankarsjo, Magnus. *William Blake and Gender*. Jefferson, NC: McFarland & Co., 2006.

Blake, William. *The Complete Poems*, ed. Alicia Suskin Ostriker. New York: Penguin, 1977.

Bruder, Helen P., and Tristanne Connolly. *Sexy Blake*. New York: Palgrave Macmillan, 2013.

Damrosch, Leopold. *Symbol and Truth in Blake's Myth*. Princeton: Princeton University Press, 1980.

Eaves, Morris. *William Blake's Theory of Art*. Princeton: Princeton University Press, 1982.

George, Diana Hume. *Blake and Freud*. Ithaca: Cornell University Press, 1980.

Matthews, Susan. *Blake, Sexuality and Bourgeois Politeness*. Cambridge: Cambridge University Press, 2011.

Mee, Jon. *Dangerous Enthusiasm: William Blake and the Culture of Radicalism in the 1790s*. Oxford: Clarendon Press, 1992.

Ostriker, Alicia Suskin. *Green Age*. Pittsburgh: University of Pittsburgh Press, 1989.

Ostriker, Alicia Suskin. *The Imaginary Lover*. Pittsburgh: University of Pittsburgh Press, 1986.

Ostriker, Alicia Suskin. *Dancing at the Devil's Party: Essays on Poetry, Politics, and the Erotic*. Ann Arbor: University of Michigan Press, 2000.

Ostriker, Alicia Suskin. "The Road of Excess: My William Blake." In *The Romantics and Us: Essays on Literature and Culture*, 67–90. New Brunswick, NJ: Rutgers University Press, 1990.

Ostriker, Alicia. *Vision and Verse in William Blake*. Madison and Milwaukee: University of Wisconsin Press, 1965.

Schuchard, Marsha Keith. *Why Mrs Blake Cried: William Blake and the Sexual Basis of Spiritual Vision*. London: Century, 2006.

Zornberg, Aviva Gottlieb. *The Murmuring Deep: Reflections on the Biblical Unconscious*. New York: Schocken Books, 2009.

DIANA HUME GEORGE

Forcing an Entry into Eternity
Alicia Ostriker's Poetry and Criticism

Writers who produce work over a period of decades, often in several genres, are difficult to discuss in a comprehensive way because when they are still living they are shape-shifters, their contributions to the life of letters ongoing. If they're generous thinkers, their perspectives both widen and deepen rather than merely narrow, so that each volume marks a subtle degree of transformation. Within that willingness to evolve, such writers also present a worldview, a philosophy, a Weltanschauung that each book both encompasses and develops, that readers, even those with their own firmly individualized versions of the Zeitgeist, will learn from. Occasionally, a fundamentally single-genre creative writer produces such a canon, with minor forays into criticism, as is the case in America with novelists such as John Crowley and Toni Morrison. But the largeness of vision I mean usually includes not only poetry or fiction, for instance, but culture criticism or scholarship or other nonfiction as meta-commentary. In America now, Adrienne Rich remains among our leading thinker/writers of this most comprehensive kind. Among British writers of the past century, Aldous Huxley might be an eclectic contender.

Alicia Suskin Ostriker, author of seventeen books of poetry and several influential critical books, including *Stealing the Language: The Emergence of Women's Poetry in America*, *Writing Like a Woman*, and *Dancing at the Devil's Party*, is also a biblical revisionist with ground-breaking studies such as *Feminist Revision and the Bible* and a generically unclassifiable meditation titled *The Nakedness of the Fathers*. Yet I first encountered her work in the 1970s with a book that at first glance seems entirely unrelated to these concerns, *Vision and Verse in William Blake*, which later led her to edit the Penguin *Blake*, an impressive work of scholarship of which most of her feminist readers are less likely to be aware. As prodigious as Harold Bloom, but with a mind more interested in contemplative growth than in intellectual strutting (she *could* do that, too), she is connected to Bloom, as to another unlikely third party in that triangulation—Allen Ginsberg—through Blake. His was the visionary impulse that first inspired her own "system," as well as Bloom's and Ginsberg's. Blake said, "I must create my own system or be enslaved by another man's." These three are the contemporary American writers who took his dictum most literally. This essay refers almost entirely to the trajectory of her volumes of poetry, with reference to her essays on poetry, and the ways in which the evolution of a transforming vision are reflected in these works. When a poet is still writing actively, we "review" the latest work, rather than reaching back to the poet's roots to gain a more comprehensive view. Having reviewed *The Little Space* (*Women's Review of Books*, December 1998) and *The Crack in Everything* (*SRPR*, Fall 1997) at the time they came out, I have different purposes here. I'll return to her middle-period work in detail, to see how the mature vision of one of our genuine women of letters developed.

Ostriker's voice is her own, yet it echoes many of the songs she first celebrated and sometimes mourned in *Stealing the Language*. Ostriker internalized the voices of other women poets, and one can hear the strains of Dickinson as well as Blake in her lines. As I wrote about *The Little Space*, her themes are those of the poet-prophet in the wilderness of the beloved and limited object world—the gendered or material world—urging herself and us to enter eternity while we can. Like Blake's, her vision of how things might be utterly changed is grounded in the anatomy of how things are. And like those women poets she internalized, she sees her own body as an extension of the natural world, and is convinced that only connection—with that world, with each other—can save us.

While Ostriker sees the need for autonomy that emerges from our culture's silencing of the feminine, her poems develop over time, with an increasing sense of urgency, the need to transcend individual ego through the power of compassion. Volume building on volume, her poems warn that our evolution into a species alienated from ourselves and each other is lethal. If the capacity for loving connection resides in us, we will have to press ourselves and each other toward it—hard, continually, hourly, against psychic forces within and outside of us that would destroy us. But any palpable sense of possible doom that pervades her poetry is dwarfed by the powers of the Lover, who is the embodied form of both eros and imagination. This is a poet in love with the world—she has said she is "in love with love"—and her poems claim that *we* can heal ourselves.

As early as "A Wild Surmise: Motherhood and Poetry," and "I Make My Psyche from My Need" (*Writing Like a Woman* 1983), Ostriker situated herself historically as a female poet. In Ostriker's case, writing like a woman meant meditating on pregnancy, birth, motherhood.

> Wasn't birth universal? Wasn't pregnancy profound? During pregnancy, for example, I believed from time to time that I understood the continuity of life and death, that my body was a city and a landscape, and that I had personally discovered the moral equivalent of war. During the final stages of labor I felt like a hero, an Olympic athlete, a figure out of Pindar, at whom a stadium should be heaving garlands. At times, again, I was overwhelmed with loathing for the ugliness of my flesh, the obscenity of life itself, all this ooze, these fluids, the grossness of it. Trying to discover a poetic form which could express such opposite revelations simultaneously, and convey the extraordinary sense of transformation from being a private individual self to being a portion of something else, I had the sense of being below the surface, where the islands are attached to each other. Other women knew what I knew. Of course they did, they always had. In that case, where were the poems? (127)

She later found the poems in Rich, Sylvia Plath, Anne Sexton, Diane Wakoski. Even buoyed up by those ambivalent mothers, she found that to celebrate motherhood she needed to confront two orthodoxies. The old masculine one forbade her to write about the body from any point of view, but especially her own. Politically militant feminist doctrine regarded motherhood as a patriarchal conspiracy. Yet central to her poetry is her belief that the advantage for a woman artist in motherhood is that it puts her "in immediate and inescapable contact with the sources of life, death, beauty, growth, corruption" (130). Fifteen years later for *The Family Track*, an academic anthology on balancing work and family, she wrote "The Maternal Mind," an essay on the connections between teaching and mothering.[1] Motherhood was also a conceptual frame for *The Mother/Child Papers* and *A Woman Under the Surface*.

The Mother/Child Papers explored the parallels between the personal and the cultural with which she said, in *Stealing the Language*, most women poets since 1960 have been concerned. Her son was born in 1970. The United States had invaded Cambodia and four students had been shot at Kent State. In this collection she contrasts the heroism of war with the heroism of giving birth. When her son is born, the doctor remarks that he will make a good soldier. "The Guard kneeled" is the death chant that takes baby sons from mothers, "hoisted up to the sky on bayonets." Birth and death intermingle in sequential exchange in this collection. The imperative of intimacy is imaged in the erotics of nursing, when

> I come the way that
> moon comes, stars, the tides,
> it is involuntary, only
>
> God knows what elastic
> pulls me to his hunger . . .

The growth of the individual infant brain is the analogue of culture established in nature. Inside his small head, everything is getting "hooked up"; a settlement is formed,

> . . . with real streets,
> a marketplace, buying and selling, and outside
> the town the ground to break,
>
> the people sowing and harvesting,
> already planning a city, and I
> want to see it, I want to.

The mother's desire to get inside the infant's mind is first sounded here, and this desire, to know the other whom one loves, to transcend flesh by delving into it, remains central in Ostriker's poetry. She will return again and again to the dear bodies of the beloveds, practicing the imperative of intimacy on those who would be known and on those who would not.

If the mother is greedy for mental knowledge, both she and the infant are greedy for each other's bodies: "You in your mouth are alive, I in my womb." From this kind of hunger, the poems move to darker places, not only in the exterior world where babies are stabbed by crazed men who were once babies themselves, but within the recesses of the maternal heart.

> You claw my skin, my nipple.
>   Am a witch. Am dry.
> Cannot endure an existence
>   chained to your cry.
> Incubus. Leech. Scream.
>   You confine me. Die.

So women are part of whatever design of darkness appalls us all. And because the son learns the capacity to hate as well as to love from the mothers as well as the fathers, she cannot know whether he will "burn forests." If he does, his mother will preserve the song of poetry, connectedness, natural abundance, beyond temporal holocaust. Responsibility for "keeping the divine vision in time of trouble" (the phrase is Blake's) must be shared by mother and child. She teaches him the "oldest, saddest story" of our species' birth and our arrival into consciousness, responsibility for which is our curse. "Shall all life / perish like us, the perfect crest subside?" The mother sees his intuition of the question even in his infancy, because he is human. "I want to tell you it is not your fault. / It is your fault." She tells her infant to keep his eye on the healing hope. "You see the silver bridge / spanning a flood?"

Another among these early poems now reads as pivotal. "Propaganda Poem: Maybe for Some Young Mamas" was the nakedly polemical address of the visiting poet to a feminist classroom of students who rejected the possibility of motherhood. We are "all of us spoiled" by time, so that ordinary men and women can seldom be gods and goddesses; but a baby, "any baby," is the "most perfect human thing you can ever touch"; the first images of deity come from the "whole mama" and the "whole little baby." The "joy that hurts nobody," the "dazzling circuit of contact without dominance," can be an act of cultural defiance rather than feminine submission, a way that powerful women ride "our tides / into the sand dunes of the public spaces." The "Postscript" goads the young women: "Come on, you daughters of bitches, do you want to live forever?"

A Woman Under the Surface teems with mortal women and men caught at the moment of becoming divine. Ostriker personalizes mythology and re-mythologizes the personal as she engages in the revisionist strategies she has found in other women poets. "I am wondering what would be a fully human / Way to express our fears" she says in "The Waiting Room," a poem clearly an extension of Elizabeth Bishop's. The poet is afraid—of and for herself, her children, her husband, her mother. Blurred or split identity, especially in connection with mothers and children, hovers like a drawn knife over *Surface*. "The Crazy Lady Speaking" demands that the poet, or any daughter, acknowledge the mad *doppelganger* within, a dangerous maternal figure externalized in the homeless, crazed females wandering the streets of cities. "I was the one in the IRT tunnel" with stockings rolled to the knee, or the one in the cafeteria at 2 a.m.: "You were afraid I might urinate on the floor." But

> You should have seen me dance in *La Sylphide*,
> In *Lac des Cygnes*. You should have seen
> My Cleopatra, my Camille, my Juliet.
> From each of their graves I rise, daughter. Embrace me.

In "Dreaming of Her," a gray-haired witch attempts violent entry into the space of the house and the psyche:

> Outside the longhouse, in a black and drizzling night,
> Although I have tightly bolted all the windows,
> A woman glides through weeds and struggles to enter.
> . . .
> All night the orange moon crosses the sky,
> Rain comes and goes, the dream repeats, repeats—
> *Mother, sometime we are going to talk*
>
> *Together, I promise*— . . .

Yet she concludes that fear revealed is nothing to be afraid of: "As if it were I, my mother, released from the black // Hunger of daughterlove." Another "Exchange" of identity is a violent, deliberately flat-toned fantasy of flight from what Plath called the "little smiling hooks" of family. The killer within the mother and wife is not an old bitch gone in the teeth, but a gorgeous water-goddess below the surface, "her powerful body shimmering, / Opalescent."

> If I dive down, if she climbs into the boat,
> Wet, wordless, she will strangle my children
> And throw their limp bodies into the stream.

Then she will drive home to the poet's door, this "magnificent naked woman, bits of sunlight / Glittering on her pubic fur," and clamp her strong arm around the husband's neck, "once for each insult // Endured." While this other within the self murders the poet's family, the poet "having exchanged with her, will swim / Away, in the cool water, out of reach." Ostriker suggests repeatedly that creativity and destruction, all psychic polarities, spring from the same sources. Many of her poems about transformations of energy take place in the fluid medium "below the surface, where the islands are attached to each other." Power and energy are morally neutral until they emanate into expression—and that expression may take the form of delight, joy, song, or it may become deformed, and mutate into destruction and sorrow.

Ostriker is also accomplished at another and contrary impulse, one I call prophetic wrath. "As in a Gallery" muses on why it is often easier to make intimate, simple contact with strangers than with those you love, "who are smeared with fear."

> I am not satisfied about that
> I pound my fist on the table! I insist
> That I am not satisfied! I put
> My fist through the wall, angrily,
>
> Making a hole. It is
> Only in my mind, but
> I am trying to force an entry—to deny
> That art is illusion, that love is illusion, that
> The amusing construction painted with the ruby hearts
> Is solid iron, in the gallery.

The wrath is genuine, but humorous, even duplicitous. She invites us to be "amused" with her and the "wine-mouthed stranger," but the hopelessness of her illusions and the necessity to "force an entry" into affirmation are serious. In this collection and the one that follows, the desire to know the beloved other becomes positively invasive, a forceful, intrusive, pick-and-shovel hacking at the walls of separation and misunderstanding between herself and people she loves. She has to do this, else the dark will swallow us all.

Yet she is willing to give as much as she demands. In "Dream: The Disclosure," she considers taking her skin off, passionately disclosing to the lover "The purple shapes fruits under my skin," the "organs in their refreshing waterfalls of blood." In return she reached "within you beginning at the / Moist cool anus" and progressed upward through bowels, stomach, heart.

This was so nice would you drink anything warm
Offered foaming to you in a wooden bowl, by outstretched hands
The juices are harmless, they are not poison, they are life.

In "Don't Be Afraid," she continues the assault of love upon all boundaries: "This is when I want to open you / Like a sweater, like a jacket // That you have kept closed."

The poet's invasive hand will caress the moment entry is forced. The powers that inhabit her are usually friendly, just as she imagines the powers that inhabit the interiors of earth, sky, and ocean would wish to be kind. In "Downstairs," death is an amicable experience, unlike what the dying man feared:

But no, there in the soil and wet
Everything and everyone showed friendship

Where he placed his hand,
Where he rested his forehead.

"Message from the Sleeper at Hell's Mouth" is a series of persona poems representing aspects of the poet's self. As she declares in *Writing Like a Woman*, Psyche is Ostriker's "awareness that I am good and cannot fail" (142). Yet Psyche kills her sisters. The sisters Psyche kills in Ostriker's version represent the split in the character of Psyche, a duality the poet acknowledges in herself. The first sister, envious and spiteful, gazes in a mirror that speaks in the voice that will later issue from Psyche's own mouth, call her to the cliff to die:

Good morning, says the mirror.
Repeat after me: Envy is a fingernail scraping a blackboard.
Self-pity is the fifth martini. Second
Best is a loser. I like your outfit.

At the end of the cycle of six poems, Psyche speaks from within her sleep:

Anyway, what is the soul
But a dream of itself? It pictures
A girl pursuing a god

Who is lovely, naked and wounded,
And in her sleep she says
Come soon, with all your arrows.

"Message from the Sleeper at Hell's Mouth" conflates many of Ostriker's other messages: a woman under the surface (of water, of sleep) dreams her deliverance from, her continual rebirth into, a world where she pursues a naked and wounded beloved who may one day be, as she may be, healed and made whole by the arrows of desire that wounded them. Ever vigilant even as she sleeps, Ostriker's Psyche is not only the sleeper at Hell's mouth, but the wakeful one at Heaven's door. She is ready for eternity the moment she can "force an entry."

The Imaginary Lover is this same Eros, and she is still Psyche, pursuing him in poetry of wakeful sleep, of dreamy alertness. The quest is clearly going to be lifelong. The beloved Eros is the human community itself. What is the soul but a dream of itself? Ostriker's enduring themes are here, her preoccupation with the body, the natural world envisioned as the matrix of life, anger and violence arising from entrapment in our gender arrangements, erotics that insist on intimacy, revisionist mythmaking—all of these fill the pages of *The Imaginary Lover*. But something else has evolved. She is now envisioning transformations so spacious that the old myths, those repositories of meaning for gender, are too confining.

Does this mean that she invents new forms, new stories, breaking free of her sources? Not at all. Rather, the transformative urge makes her return endlessly to the ordinary, phenomenal world, inhabited by women and men like herself, where the real work must be done. To envision how things might change, her poems seem to say that she must ever-more-clearly sharpen her sight of how things are. Even after demystification, mystery remains. The tone of many of these poems is essentially elegiac, and the collective speaker of the poems is writing what might best be called wisdom literature, which is how many readers seem to respond to the genre she will next turn to, meditations on the Bible in *The Nakedness of the Fathers*.

New questions occur to the poet/speaker. "What was the first animal / People recognized as beautiful?" In "Horses," her answer brings us back to individual human sources,

Our parents, their whiskered nostrils, those sharp
Tunnels into eternity, and even

Now when they stop, bent
To our oated hands, muzzles so soft, the horses

Are never tamed, never entirely tamed.

With the dead man in the hospital, the poet sings "liberty's song," while his wishes "are flying apart like spores / Over his white eyebrows." If a marriage must "Dissolve, in Slow Motion" even as the observer would like to snap it like a twig to save the sufferers, she stands inside the wrecked laboratory to ask, "Has something been measured? / It all gets thrown away." When "The Contest" results in a woman shooting her lover with a tiny gun like a "rigid hummingbird," she tosses the pistol away and gets back in bed, "where it is her own / Brain that the slug is in." These people are pursued by their own desire, and by the unknown desires of other and multiple powers, some friendly, some vicious. "The Woman Who Ran Away" asks:

> Will I die soon? Why am I alive,
> My body leaking heat,
> Words of praise misting my lips?

Voices call the "Widow in a Stone House" to come to nothingness:

> And cold excites me, it is hysterical
> And greedy, it clangs and ripples like fat

> Moon slices sliding across lakewater
> In a Magritte painting, it is an owl

> Dropped on a chainlink fence, that I am watching . . .

Just when she might be safely embedded in life—"Today I feel as if I have eaten fire"—the cloudy voices say: "*Listen. We're trying to find you. / Listen. We think we can see you.*"

In "Listen," she wants the gods "Who have eluded me / All my life, or whom I have eluded" to invite her daughter "regularly / To their lunches and jazz recitals." It is only "A Question of Time" before grown daughter and mother should get time off for good behavior "If I behave well, which / I do not plan to do." The other familial relationship through which the poet seeks redemption is marriage. She knows that in all our bodily and psychic injuries "we begin to rehearse our deaths," and that "Every portion of our useful bodies / Will forsake us" ("The Hurt Eye"). But in that body and the mind it houses—one of the "authorized dualities" of our culture that she tries to imagine into wholeness, into marriage—reside her hope. The marriage poems here are mind / body conversations in which the poet is still "Wanting All":

What more do I want, then, why
Do I prowl the basement, why
Do l reach for your inside
Self as you shut it
Like a trunkful of treasures? *Wait,*
I cry, as the lid slams on my fingers.

"Years" is a continuation of this almost obsessive theme, in which the poet acknowledges that "I have broken into you like a burglar / And you've set your dogs on me." This husband is a monument she has climbed, "gasping, / For the exercise and the view."

Like many feminists, Ostriker's urge to transform includes resurrection of the dead sister-mother-artists whose lives were cut short or unrecognized or thwarted. "Surviving," about Paula Modersohn-Becker, wants to learn from all the broken and lost mothers. Another poem that asks to learn something useful from waste and carnage is "The War of Men and Women," which finds, like Adrienne Rich's poems on the same subjects, that every failure between men and women is the failure of the imagination to "join our life with the dangerous life of the other." This poem traces the course of the frozen river between men and women, acknowledging rage against other women, the desire to kill an innocent male friend, the hope that we might blast away our "fossil selves," for "Everyone who has been in eternity knows / It is not discipline / It is sudden surrender" that gets us there. The poem ends with the war still on, the self and the other still crippled, for as she says in "While Driving North," "Mostly the land records catastrophe. / Literature the same." Because it explains the "breaking of pentameter," and why "free verse" had to occur at the moment it did, far better than any historical account I've read, I teach this poem the first day of my modern poetry course.

But deadpan formulation styled as a flat confession, while true enough of many poems here, is also a lie, or at best a half-truth. The struggle against catastrophe is what Ostriker's own literature records, and the reimaginings that might be simpler. Consider that ultimate catastrophe, death. We hear the beating of its wings throughout this collection, but then "Death Is Only" this: "The soul in its rowboat, pulling away" through wide water, taking "Great gulps of the sky." For years the soul has been frightened,

But why? What did it fear?
It can't remember.

While Ostriker frequently pauses to admire the view afforded us by "this wounded world that is our bride," the tone of her poetry is increasingly urgent and insistent. Important work remains to be done, and there is little time to accomplish it. The horses are beautiful, and although she cannot stop for death, she knows it will kindly stop for her, and for all she loves. The horses' heads are toward eternity. Eternity is available to us from within this world if we force an entry, and the dead are "continually beseeching us" to "heal ourselves."

Green Age (1989) continues her spiritual quest at a high pitch of tension, abhorring the barriers to mutual compassion. She civilly insists that we love each other, believing it's all that can possibly save us. Late in the volume, she writes of the beloved Friend that Rumi called God. As one would now expect from Ostriker, the Friend is in people around her, in family members, in her students, even in complete strangers. The Rumi poems are worthy of their source of inspiration, but they are her own—original, American, Jewish, feminist. "The Death Ghazals" is addressed to the God of her fathers, and of *The Nakedness of the Fathers* and *Feminist Revision and the Bible*, books now interwoven with the subject matter of her poetry. Speaking to the god who presides over all our human battlefields, she demands, "Does your smeared forehead out-top the gracious mountains?" "A Meditation in Seven Days" once again forces entry into the sacred patriarchal place. Although she is "fearful," her "hand is on the latch / I am the woman, and about to enter."

If there was something slightly muted about *Green Age*, that does not show in the selections from it for *The Little Space*, a superb volume. Ostriker returned to her fullest powers in *The Crack in Everything* (1996), where elegiac tone is wedded to contagious joy. At last the poet who has been warning us Cassandra-like about death all around us, the need to get it right pretty *damned* soon, has faced that specter herself in the form of breast cancer. In excerpts from "The Mastectomy Poems," wit wins over despair, as in "Mastectomy," where she asks her doctor, "Was I succulent? Was I juicy?" In her tones are Sexton's fairy tales and Plath's hospital dirges, but this is also ripe Ostriker, and *Crack* is full of her, happily weary of well-meaning questions, "bookbag on my back" and running out the door as "winter turns to spring" ("Epilogue: Nevertheless").

In *The Little Space*, the "Uncollected and New" section is short, only nine pieces, half of them poems about works of art. In "From the Prado Rotunda: Family of Charles IV, and Others" she wonders about Goya's motives, or at least his effect on us. Is he "leading us by the hand like babes / To worship the abject monstrous because it exists . . . ?" Perhaps. And what does it mean if we find these images ravishing, beautiful? Then we must consider our complicities and realize that we transform everything we see into a projection of our own desire:

> The painting is never what is *there*,
> It throbs with the mystery
> Of your own sick-to-death soul
> Which demands, like everything alive,
> Love.

It is rare to find a discerning critic whose primary motive seems to be appreciation of what she synthesizes and analyzes, yet "love" is also an accurate descriptor for the tone of Ostriker's criticism in the essays collected in *Dancing at the Devil's Party*, written over a period of years. She doesn't see much point in writing about poetry one doesn't find worthwhile. So the essays here record her favorite subjects—Blake and Whitman, Elizabeth Bishop and Sharon Olds, Maxine Kumin, Lucille Clifton, and most recently, Allen Ginsberg. These essays are a joy to read because Ostriker is widely read, a genuine intellectual, a compleat woman of letters for our time, and an exceptionally graceful prose writer.

Her own way of expressing why she writes about poetry she likes says it best. In the title essay, the phrase "The Devil's Party" echoes again her first major poetic influence, the Bigdaddy named Blake, not the Nobodaddy named Milton—whom she also, more than incidentally, both knows and loves, as did Blake, who was talking about Milton, after all, when he said it in the first place.

> Wit, grace, passion, eloquence, playfulness, compression, vitality, freshness. A voice that is at once the poet's voice and the voice of a time, a nation, a gender. The many, mysteriously funneled through the one: not I, not I, but the wind that blows through me . . . I prefer the word "love" to the word "evaluate." Bring out number, weight, and measure in a year of dearth, says Blake. I find "love" more reliable than "evaluate." First I see what I love, then I try to understand it. (6)

Notes

A version of this essay was first published in *Spoon River Poetry Review* (abbreviated as *SRPR*) in 2000. Numbers of Ostriker's publications are among the updates in this version.

1. *The Family Track: Keeping Your Faculties while You Mentor, Nurture, Teach, and Serve*, eds. Constance Coiner and Diana Hume George (Urbana-Champaign: University of Illinois Press, 1998), 3–7.

MARILYN HACKER

Tectonic Shifts, on *The Crack in Everything*

Alicia Ostriker's work joins the humanitarian's unalienated will to ameliorate suffering and share what's of value (which energizes progressive political engagement) to the humanist's hunger to re-engage with and continually redefine intellectual (specifically literary, also spiritual) traditions: the pedagogical passion. She is a Blake scholar and a Bible scholar, a feminist critic whose work continues to germinate a wider-branching, inclusive literary purview, a Jew whose writings are informed by, while they interrogate, that heritage and history. She is a mother and a teacher. She is also an important American poet, whose writing is enriched, and enriches its readers, by all those sometimes conflicting identities.

The Crack in Everything is her eighth collection of poems (and her thirteenth book). Ostriker is not a "difficult" poet, demanding of the reader a primary concern with the construction (or deconstruction) of literary edifices: she is a Socratic poet, who engages the reader in complex examinations by means of simple questions, deceptively simple declarative sentences.

> I picked the books to come along with me
> On this retreat at the last moment
>   . . .
> In Chicago, Petersburg, Tokyo, the dancers
> Hit the floor running
>   . . .
> We say things in this class. Like why it hurts.
>   . . .
> I called him fool, she said
> It just slipped out

A series of homages to other ordinary extraordinary women frames the book's first half. Two dramatic monologues, spoken by a middle-class and a working-class woman, confronting the end (or not) of

---

A version of this essay was published in *The Nation*, 2 May 1997.

marriage, are followed, mirrored, by two magnificent portraits of known artists—the painter Alice Neel and the poet May Swenson—in which Ostriker meticulously details the way various ordinarinesses can coalesce into genius. After a vivid introductory stanza in which all the senses are called to witness, in counterpoint with a litany of American brand names, Neel, quintessential urban American painter, speaks (through the poet) for herself:

You got to understand, this existence is it,
I blame nobody, I just paint, paint is thicker than water,
Blood, or dollars. My friends and and neighbors are made
Of paint, would you believe it, paintslabs and brushstrokes
Right down to the kishkes, as my grandfather would say.
Like bandaged Andy, not smart enough to duck.

Palette knife jabs, carnation, ochre, viridian.

She speaks and continues, relentlessly, to recount her descent into and emergence from mental illness.

Swenson's portrait is structured on word-and-eye-perfect observation: of a tortoise, which generates the image of the child-poet examining the animal, and the mature poet's own not untortoise-like, equally cannily observed physical presence.

"Amphibian, crustacean?" Ostriker asks, to begin, and concludes, "It's friendly. Really a mammal." A modest inference to which Swenson would readily have assented, as she'd have been pleased to be glimpsed in her own naturalist's glass. These strains meet in the book's long centerpiece, "The Book of Life," addressed to sculptor Sheila Solomon, whose work readers won't know as they do Neel's and Swenson's. The theme of the poet's and sculptor's correspondences and their differences, as artists, as friends, as Jews, as parents, interweaves with descriptions of the sculptor's work and workplace, and with the story of a third friend, who died of cancer in early middle age:

You started the eight-foot goddess
The year Cynthia spent dying,
The same year you were sculpting
Her small bald head
Fretting you couldn't get
The form.

In five sections, seven dense pages, "The Book of Life" is more like the notebook (writers' "books of life") from which a complex poem might be drawn. "Figurative sculpture is dead," the sculptor is told, but persists in her own figurative, majestic vision. This poem, with its doubled or tripled levels of narration and description, left me wishing for what I equate with the figurative in poetry: the fixed structure of accentual-syllabic form to order its plunges and ascents through the sculptor's studio and garden, the friends' shared history. Ostriker is, in general, a poet whose formal strategies inspire confidence, and seem the outer manifestation of the poem's intentions, whether in the Sapphic echoes of the triplet stanzas of the epithalamium "Extraterrestrial," the clear-cut free-verse couplets of the May Swenson tribute, or the Augustan rhymed pentameter, witty and elegiac, of "After the Reunion."

Ostriker is a teacher by vocation, one feels, not just through economic necessity, a poet/scholar who teaches not only "creative writing" but the creative reading that sustains the republic of letters. Many poets and novelists teach. Ostriker, along with Toi Derricotte and Marie Ponsot, is one of the few who has written about, recognized, and re-created the pedagogic relationship as one of the quintessentially human connections, as fit a subject for poetry as erotic love or the changes spring rings on a meadow. Her students, as individuals or cohered into a class, are present in a group of these poems, where the dynamic that fuels a class's work together is examined not as new tapes but a multivocal conversation, a collective expedition:

> All semester they brought it back
> A piece at a time, like the limbs of Osiris.

Generous as she is, Ostriker can permit herself the rueful professorial aside that the one student who "gets" Emily Dickinson, after the teacher's inspired cadenza on her poems, is "the boy / Who'd had four years of Latin / In high school and loved Virgil." Activist that she has always been, Ostriker cannot view the university in a vacuum, peopled only by students and teachers. "Lockout," the poem that opens the university sequence, is spoken largely by a middle-aged Latino security guard, aware of how the imported hegemony of English has inflected his life and the lives of the continent's native peoples.

The contemplative poem "After Illness" makes graceful reference to gratuitous, inevitable bodily destiny, different but equally mortal for each individual:

What is a dance without some mad randomness
Making it up? Look, getting sick
Was like being born,

They singled you out from among the others
With whom you were innocently twirling,
Doing a samba across the cumulonimbus,

They said *you*, they said *now*.

Three pages, two sections later, still in a cropped triplet stanza, the
poet/speaker refers to "my mastectomy"—but in a subordinate
clause of a sentence whose conditional object, and objective, is
"mourning" and "feeling," counterbalanced by imagined indul-
gence of an improvident infatuation; the conclusion is that any
consciously determined subject matter of meditation "By defini-
tion isn't it!" In this elegant philosophical play, mastectomy seems to
enter almost offhandedly into the discourse, until the reader realizes
how it informs the earlier stanzas about the dance of randomness,
the falling into the body of illness as we've fallen into our bodies at
birth. The balance between the raw, unresolved mourning for Cyn-
thia in "The Book of Life" and this almost ludic intrusion of the
harsh word "mastectomy" with its vulnerable "my" prepares the
reader for the book's concluding and conclusive achievement, "The
Mastectomy Poems," a twelve-poem sequence.

In the book's preceding sections, Ostriker has displayed a virtuoso
register of styles, voices, forms: the dramatic monologue/word-
portrait; the aphoristic or fable-like narrative in meter and rhyme; the
pedagogical "I" addressing a plural "thou"; the quotidian anecdotal
that shifts subtly into the meditative or the surreal. She deploys all of
these in "The Mastectomy Poems" to create a mosaic of a woman's
changing inner and outer life as she undergoes this ordeal that has
become so horrifyingly common as to resemble a rite of passage. All
the while, given the book's structure, in the augmented formal echoes
of its preceding themes, she reiterates as subtext that the breast cancer
survivor is, chastened and changed, the same woman, the same artist
and citizen, that she was before—she who praises other women (here,
a breast surgeon) in the exercise of their vocations:

I shook your hand before I went.
Your nod was brief, your manner confident,
A ship's captain, and there I lay, a chart
Of the bay, no reefs, no shoals.

a sensual/social woman:

> . . . I told a man *I've resolved*
> *To be as sexy with one breast*
> *As other people are with two*
> And he looked away

a lyric economist of meter and rhyme:

> And now the anesthesiologist,
> Tells something reassuring to my ear—
> And a red moon is stripping to her waist—
> *How good it is, not to be anywhere*

a teacher and member of the academic community:

> First classes, the sun is out, the darlings
> Troop in, my colleagues
> Tell me I look normal. I am normal.

Always, though, underneath the surface, under the "Black and red China silk jacket," is the shocked, transformed body, the "skinny stripe," "short piece of cosmic string" of the mastectomy scar, at once sign of escape and memento mori.

Omnipresent, too, the scar's double, is the lost breast, also with a double significance, first as instrument of pleasure, self-contained sustenance, bodily benignity, badge of responsible womanhood: "my right guess, my true information," transformed into a kind of time bomb, storehouse of explosives, inert but dangerous matter:

> Jug of star fluid, breakable cup—
> Someone shoveled your good and bad crumbs
> Together into a plastic container . . .
> For breast tissue is like silicon.

And the breast, or the ghost breast, marks mortality now even more than the scar:

> *Carry me, mama.* Sweetheart,
> I hear you, I will come.

"The River" concludes: the generative constant rescue mission of maternity thus transformed into the poet's prescience of death.

Abruptly, the sequence's next, last poem begins and ends with the speaker back in the quotidian world of work and talk: "The bookbag on my back, I'm out the door"—a teacher again, with the vivacity and accouterments of a young student in her self-description. "Winter turns to spring / The way it does," and she unthinkingly answers the anxious *"How are you feeling"* with anecdotes about family and work. The "woman under the surface" is back on the surface, in her disguise as an ordinary worker bee, an ordinariness like that which camouflages the genius of Swenson and Neel in their poem-portraits. But this section is titled "Epilogue"—which gives us the double message that, despite the brisk exit line, the poem's real conclusion is the haunted one of "The River."

One section of "The Mastectomy Poems" has an epigraph—referring to "an ordinary woman"—from a poem by Lucille Clifton. Clifton too was treated for breast cancer, a few years after Ostriker. Some, only some, of the contemporary American writers who are living with, or who have succumbed to, breast cancer are, in no particular order: Pat Parker, Audre Lorde, Susan Sontag, Maxine Kumin, Eve Kosofsky Sedgwick, Penelope Austin, Edith Konecky, Hilda Raz, Patricia Goedicke, June Jordan, myself; black, white, Jewish; fat, thin, and middling; lesbian, straight, and middling; childless and multiparous "And"—to borrow the title of a poem by Melvin Dixon about friends lost to AIDS—"These Are Just a Few."

The Crack in Everything: Is it a shift in the earth's tectonic plates, the purposeful Zen flaw in a ceramic vase that individualizes its perfection, the long pink keloid ridge on a newly flat chest? All of the above. This is not a polemic, a book with an aim, a recovery manual. The crack reaffirms the poet's unique and contradictory role, at once storyteller and witness, she who makes of language not a prison but a prism, refracting and re-combining the spectrum of human possibilities.

MARION HELFER WAJNGOT

"Well, Burn My Bush!"
*Alicia Ostriker in Dialogue
with Biblical Narrative*

The title—"Well, þurn my bush"—is taken from one of the last pages of Alicia Ostriker's *The Nakedness of the Fathers: Biblical Visions and Revisions* (251). The second-to-last section of this book, "Intensive Care," is a futuristic fiction about a dying God in an intensive care ward, and the exclamation "Well, burn my bush" is the reaction of a woman journalist to her colleague's comments on the situation. With its allusion to the biblical narrative of Moses and the burning bush (Exodus 3), the line is characteristic of the hermeneutic method of the entire book, and this in turn is modeled on the Jewish midrash tradition of Bible interpretation. This exegetical tradition allows Ostriker to hark back to a text written between 2,000 and 3,000 years ago while meditating on and being intensely involved with problems of the late twentieth century. When the image of the burning bush reappears toward the end of the book, imbued with obvious sexual overtones, it serves as a node for some of the central themes and issues of Ostriker's work: the identity of the Jewish feminist as part of the tradition and of the modern world, the woman as midrashist, the woman as writer, as reader, as protagonist of her own text, as creator of her own myth. In addition, the burning bush, the visual sign of divine interference in the liberation of the people of Israel from slavery, becomes a symbol for the values of liberty, compassion, and human rights.

Especially central to the work of American Jewish woman, poet, critic, writer, and professor Alicia Suskin Ostriker are the terms "American," "Jewish," and "woman." Ostriker grapples with being a woman in modern America through her Jewish heritage, and with this heritage through her feminism. Each chapter, indeed each of the biblical texts she works with, becomes a node for these different strands in her thinking and in her being. In the preface Ostriker declares that she intends "*The Nakedness of the Fathers* to speak across

Jewish/Christian boundaries, across male/female boundaries, and across the boundaries that separate past from present, daily life from eternity, and the life of the body from that of the spirit" (xv). The boundary most clearly to be crossed in this work is that between male and female, but for Ostriker this move has to take place within the Jewish tradition. As a starting point for this theme, Ostriker establishes her Jewishness:

> Could I despise the drops of blood in my body? To deny my Judaism would be like denying the gift of life, the reality of sorrow, the pleasures of learning and teaching. To reject Judaism would be to surrender an idea of justice inseparable from compassion. (6)

For Ostriker the tie to Judaism is inescapable, as she asserts in this highly personal text. The aspects of Judaism, or of Jewishness, that she finds it impossible to reject are those of some of its most central ideas, ideas handed down through the generations in an unbroken chain of learning and teaching, teaching and learning. How the idea of justice is linked to the image of the burning bush will become clear. For now, let us note that Judaism, like life, is accepted as a gift, received and treasured, but far from unproblematic:

> To the rest of the world the Jew is marginal. But to Judaism I am marginal. Am woman, unclean. Am Eve. Or worse, am Lilith. Am illiterate. Not mine the arguments of Talmud, not mine the centuries of ecstatic study, the questions and answers twining minutely like vines around the living Word, not mine the Kaballah, the letters of the Hebrew alphabet dancing as if they were attributes of God. (6)[1]

The writer is Jewish but, coming from an orthodox background, she is prevented from approaching Jewish texts because she is a woman. In spite of this sense of exclusion, however, Ostriker has appropriated the heritage, its texts and its methods. Hers are "the questions and answers twining minutely like vines around the living Word," that is, the search for meaning in the scripture that belongs to the hermeneutic tradition called midrash. The word *midrash* refers both to a genre of rabbinical commentary, and to compilations of such interpretations, as well as to individual commentaries. Its origin is in the Hebrew verb *darash*, which means to search or investigate.[2] Concerning the rabbis' explorations of the text of the Bible, the word means interpretation. The modern midrash scholar

Jacob Neusner ascribes three dimensions, or functions, to midrash. The first is "as explanation of meaning imputed to particular verses of Scripture," the second "as a mode of stating important propositions, syllogisms of thought, in conversation with . . . sustained passages of Scripture," and the third "as a way of retelling stories that imparts new immediacy to those stories" (*Invitation to Midrash* 3–4). Midrash is a search for meaning that on the one hand is an amplification or explanation of the biblical text, while on the other hand it imparts meaning through that text to what we might call the baffling present narrative of existence. Although Ostriker works in all three modes in *The Nakedness of the Fathers*, she stresses in particular that of retelling the story. She turns to the biblical narrative, amplifies it so that the text gains a fresh meaning, and applies it to her immediate surrounding.

This kind of writing demonstrates the flexibility both of the Biblical text and of the midrashic method. The classical midrash material is extremely diversified, consisting of comments on and discussions of legal, linguistic, literary, historical, and ethical issues, as well as theological matters. Ostriker's work has a similar generic diversity. Her text is a mixture of expository prose, poetry, poetic prose, and autobiography; it is at times dryly argumentative, at times dreamlike. Her text interacts not only with the Bible but also with texts of all kinds that belong to the cultural heritage of an American Jewish woman.

A special feature is the tradition of narrative exegesis developed within midrash. Indeed, in everyday language the word "midrash" has come to mean a tale. As Ostriker says in the preface to her book, the midrashic narratives are "stories based on Biblical stories, composed not for a narrow audience of scholars, but for an entire community" (xii–xiii). The stories, or parables, are parallels or extensions of Biblical narratives. At times the meaning is expanded through the introduction of a minor detail, at times a completely different story is told, with different characters at a different point in history and with only a seemingly remote link to the scriptural text.

Each chapter of *The Nakedness of the Fathers* is introduced by quotations that look like epigraphs: in each case a biblical quotation is followed by one from a later work. This is not uncommon in scholarly writing, but here the quotes serve as more than illustration or amplification (a sign of the writer's learning)—each one is the starting point for the chapter, which is indeed a *drash*, an interpretation of the quoted passage. For the second, additional or complementary quote of each chapter, Ostriker draws on sources from a variety of areas and periods, including twentieth-century poetry, fiction, philosophy, feminist literary theory, and science.

The book as a whole is introduced by a quotation from the prophet Joel, which serves as a justification for the presumption of writing Bible interpretation: "It shall come to pass afterward that I will pour out my spirit upon all flesh; your sons and daughters shall prophesy, your old men shall dream dreams, and your young men shall see visions; and also upon the servants and the handmaids . . . will I pour out my spirit" (Joel 2:28–29). The vision is all-inclusive, making no distinction of age, class, or gender, and serves to justify a woman's attempts to also see beyond the word. By encompassing within its vision a bridging of the gap between genders within the Jewish tradition, the quotation does what Ostriker aspires to do.

The male world of study and scholarship, all of what is "not mine" for Ostriker, is what the image of "the nakedness of the fathers" represents: that to which a daughter is denied access. The phrase is immediately associated with Noah's nakedness when he is drunk and seen by his son Ham (Genesis 9:21–25), and with Lot's nakedness when his daughters sleep with him (Genesis 19:30–38). Both of these incidents appear in Ostriker's work, the former as a short section entitled "The Father's Nakedness," the latter expanded as a sexual fantasy narrated by one of the daughters, "The Cave." Seeing such nakedness entails transgression, passing the boundaries of the forbidden.[3] In a footnote to her discussion of the book of Ruth, Ostriker remarks that

> as a Moabitess she is descended from one of Lot's daughters who lay with Lot incestuously—"Moab" means "from the father"— and indeed Ruth's seduction of the paternal Boas (who calls her "daughter") is like an idyllic pastoral replay (redemption?) of the story of Lot's daughters. For Torah loves the breaking of boundaries, we see it again and again. (175)[4]

The image of "[uncovering] the father's nakedness" (8) thus suggests the specific transgression of incest. In Ostriker's work the idea of uncovering the father is linked to that of "entering the tents"—the name of the first section of the book. Both of these images are metaphors of transgression, or at least of passing a boundary into the private, the forbidden. This is linked to the idea of the text, and the study of the text, as forbidden ground to women. For Ostriker "to enter the tents/texts, invade the sanctuary, uncover the father's nakedness" are all essentially one act, an act of love for the father to which she is impelled by her Jewish blood (8–9). Through the sensuous quality of her prose, Ostriker focuses on the metaphorical sense of the excessive love of an incestuous relationship as a fruitful relation with a progenitor who passes on the seeds of learning and tradition.

The metaphor of "entering the tents" stands for entering the texts, becoming one in a union almost sexual with the inherited scriptures and commentaries. Ostriker wishes "*to make each story open to me, as I climb into and into it. To make each story open, as I climb down into its throat*" (8). The throat, of course, is the source of sound, of voice, of the word, but the images of penetration are suggestive of sexuality. Kabbalah, Jewish mysticism, sees a connection of sexuality as well as of spiritual energies between the throat and the genitals (Parfitt 123). Entering the tents is entering the text. Entering the space where intimacy takes place may be a way to "invade the sanctuary," just as within the kabbalistic tradition sexual union may be a way to spiritual elevation. Conversely, "entering the tent/text" is a metaphor for the reproduction that becomes the history of a people, and for the foremost function of the fathers, which is to be exactly that—fathers. Ostriker traces the succession of patriarchs (somewhat arbitrarily), of biblical fathers, beginning with Adam, Cain and Abel, Noah and his sons, Abraham, Isaac, and Jacob. Long chapters are dedicated to Joseph, to David, and to Solomon. As she follows the story of the people transformed from myth to legend to history, she traces the transformation of the patriarchal role from that of father and begetter to that of king and warrior; from being the father of a family, a tribe, to being the father of a nation, a political leader.

But nakedness also conveys a sense of defenselessness, of the vulnerability of the un-clothed or un-closed person. Naked is someone stripped of the clothing that civilization or climate impels us to wear, but it is also a person exposed, seen for what he or she really is. Ostriker attempts to expose the biblical fathers, and to convey her own responses to their stories both from a sociopolitical-historical point of view and from a more personal perspective. Her approach is dynamic, entering the consciousness of biblical figures and making them real, bringing them to life. Moreover, "the fathers" of her title refers to her own father and grandfathers, to whom the book is dedicated and whose stories she tells, as well as to the patriarchs.

Ostriker's text is thus among other things a mixture of fiction and family history, and these as well as the other kinds of writing included are to be read as scripture commentary, as exegesis. The qualities of midrashic hermeneutics that make this kind of writing possible have been described by David Stern in *Midrash and Theory*:

> The typical midrashic predilection for multiple interpretations rather than for a single truth behind the text; its irresistible desire to tease out the nuances of Scripture rather than use interpretation to close them off; and, most of all, the way midrashic discourse mixes text and commentary, violating the boundaries between them and intentionally blurring their differences, flourishing precisely in the greyish no-man's-land between exegesis and literature. (3–4)

The openness of midrash to interpretive multiplicity, its acceptance of polysemy, originates in the view of the Torah expressed in the midrash, which says that God looked into the Torah and then created the world (*Genesis Rabbah* 1:1). The Torah, the Word, is in this view originary, a kind of blueprint for the creation of the world, that contains in itself all potential interpretation.[5]

Because interpretation originates in the scriptural text, it derives its authority from that text, and consequently all interpretations are considered equally valid. Unrelated or even contradictory interpretations can stand side by side, without canceling one another. This, the Jewish approach to scripture, is metonymic in the sense that each new interpretation, each new narrative, is added to those that come before, linked by association, and forming what Susan Handelman calls "the succession of links on the chain of metonymic signification, a chain where signified and signifier do not merge: one approaches the other only by interpretive approximation, and identity is constituted by positioning along this chain within the play of its polysemy" (110). Interpretation, then, whether in the form of commentary or narrative, is cumulative rather than successive. This is evident in Ostriker's references to the accumulated scholarship and cultural heritage, where her own contribution forms but another link.

The image of the burning bush is an example of how Ostriker works with the principles of midrashic hermeneutics. In the final section of the book several lines of exegesis converge in the reiterated appearance of the image, lines that draw together the issues of human rights, of the liberation of (Jewish) women, of the male and female aspects of the spiritual presence in the world. But earlier in the text the writer has already established a platform consisting of the interpretations of others, as well as her own, in the chapter that deals with Moses, "The Nursing Father." Like all other chapters in the book, this one opens with a biblical quotation. This quotation, which serves as a base text for the chapter, is where the burning bush first appears, in Ostriker's text and in the Bible:

And the Angel of the Lord appeared unto him in a flame of fire out of the midst of a bush: and he looked, and, behold, the bush burned with fire, and the bush was not consumed. (Exodus 3:2) (121)

This is followed by a quotation from *Exodus and Revolution* by Michael Walzer, which points to the central role of this particular narrative as a source of other narratives and as a justification for the uprising against tyranny and bondage: "This story made it possible to tell other stories." The story is that of the Exodus from Egypt, and the liberation of the people of Israel from slavery. If we read on, the biblical text goes on to say that God speaks to Moses from the burning bush, introducing himself as the God of his ancestors and saying: "I have indeed seen the affliction of My people, who are in Egypt, and I have heard their cries because of their slave-drivers; for I have been aware of their sufferings. Now I have come down to rescue them from the hand of Egypt and to bring them up from this land to a good and spacious land, a land that can flow with milk and honey" (Exodus 3:7–8).[6] This is the promise associated with the burning bush, the promise of release from servitude and of a land flowing with milk and honey. But the burning bush, read as a metaphor for God's presence and the spiritual nature of the enterprise of the exodus, can also be seen as a symbol for all liberation from suppression and slavery.

At the end of the chapter Ostriker reverts to the general, universal issue of slavery and freedom in a paragraph which is widely and wildly intertextual, referring to pioneer American, African-American, British, and Jewish sources of her cultural heritage. The passage is the climax of a section on the promised land, the promised land that has become—America. "*I write*," says Ostriker, "*in American space and Jewish time*" (128). Liberty and responsibility are the themes of this powerful passage:

The promised land really exists, it really doesn't, are we there yet. Borders unspecified, we will know when we've arrived. Profusely fertile, agriculturally a heartland; good also for grazing; room for cities. Are we there yet. The land of opportunity, these truths to be self-evident, it is necessarily elsewhere from sea to shining sea. No more auction block. Take this hammer, carry it to the captain, tell him I'm gone. Emancipate yourself from mental slavery. If you are not for yourself who is for you, if you are for yourself alone what are you, and if not now, when. Keep your hand on that plow, hold on. No more sin and suffering, no pharaoh, no king, one man one vote, are we there yet, no grinding the faces of the poor, are we there yet, no bribing of judges, are we there yet.

An impossible place, let freedom ring in it. We've been to the mountain. We've seen the land: a terrain of the imagination, its hills skipping for joy. How long, we say, we know our failure in advance, nobody alive will set foot in it. (142–43)

These stories, Ostriker implies, are some of those that the narrative of the burning bush and the Exodus from Egypt allows us to tell: the story of the *Mayflower*, the story of the African-American population, its suffering and its struggle for freedom, the American Revolution, as well as the nonrevolutionary transformations of social systems toward democracy, etc., etc. Through fragments of songs and spirituals, political declarations and slogans, the passage echoes with the biblical verses from Exodus that speak of the land where the people will be brought once they have been released from their bondage, once they have been to the mountain to receive the Torah, once all of those who were slaves in Egypt have died. The quotation in the middle of the paragraph, "*If you are not for yourself who is for you, if you are for yourself alone what are you, and if not now, when*" is ascribed to the first-century Jewish sage Hillel and is known to every Jewish child with an even vaguely traditional upbringing. It is a link in an exegetical chain, which begins with the message of the burning bush, the basic promise of freedom, and passes via the concept of righteousness, which Ostriker expresses as "*an idea of justice inseparable from compassion*" (6), to an insistence on personal responsibility.

In the last chapter, the exclamation "Well, burn my bush" has an obvious sexual connotation, but its echoing of the burning bush in Exodus refers it straight back to the heritage. The utterance hovers between the vulgar expression of skepticism conveyed by the structure of the colloquialism (cf. "kiss my ass") and an expression of deepest awe and faith. Essential, however, is the possessive—*my* bush; this is an insistence on the inclusion of the woman within the spiritual aspect of the heritage. But not only will the bush burn and emit its spiritual message also to the woman; as a sexual metaphor it forms part of the transgressive dimension this implies for Ostriker.

The exclamation comes at the end of a chapter that depicts a dying God, or as one of the women suggests, a pregnant God about to give birth. The male God is not only endowed with human failings and frailty but also with the female potential to take part in creation through childbearing. This wildly humorous fiction is followed by a serious address to the traditional female aspect of God in the last chapter, a poem entitled "A Prayer to the Shekhinah." In Jewish philosophy the Shekhinah is God's presence or immanence in the world, appearing in the liturgy in such phrases as *tachat kanfei ha-Shekhinah*—"under the wings of the Shekhinah." In the complicated theology of the Kabbalah, however, the Shekhinah represents the feminine principle of the divine world or of the godhead.[7] Here the idea of the disturbed unity of the masculine principle and the Shekhinah also appears: the true unity of God has been destroyed by the sins of Israel and by the evil power, resulting in the exile of the Shekhinah, exiled herself or, in another version, having followed the people of Israel into exile. Human life, or Jewish life, ought to be part of an endeavor to mend the world (the concept of *tikkun olam*) and thereby to effect the return of the Shekhinah, and the reunion of the masculine and the feminine principles of the divinity.

Although Ostriker insists that she is excluded from Jewish scholarship, she includes herself almost aggressively in that tradition. In answer to the fathers of the title, the final section is named "Though She Delay: The Return of the Mothers." The first stanza or section of the final poem, "A Prayer to the Shekhinah," takes the shape of a rewriting of a prayer from the liturgy for the Day of Atonement: "You are our father and we are your children." In Ostriker's version this becomes "Come be our mother   we are your young ones" (253). Just as Ostriker advocates an appropriation of the heritage by Jewish women, she cries out for the feminine aspect of the divinity to become uppermost. Most important, the innovative, the creative, in Ostriker's text arises in the zone where Judaism and feminism meet, where the inheritance becomes a meaningful present. Hers is a forceful taking over of the heritage, in spite of or because of her womanhood, a unifying in herself of the Jewish woman, the American poet, and the excluded scholar.

In my reading of *The Nakedness of the Fathers* it is in relation to these ideas that the two symbolic aspects of the burning bush coincide. With its evocation of the female genitals, the nakedness of the woman/mother, the bush must be part of the uncovering and must "burn" in passion for the act of knowing to take place ("to know" in biblical Hebrew, as in Western translations, is of course a euphemism for sexual intercourse). The burning bush is thus a metaphor for liberation in general, and for the transgressive, the revolutionary, the female intrusion into the traditionally male in particular, including the traditionally male domains of learning, writing, and commenting. It symbolizes both the transgression of entering the tents and uncovering the nakedness of the fathers, and a belief in a divine motivation behind human ethics. Thus the burning for freedom and justice, and the burning for learning and knowledge, entail uncovering the male *and* the female nakedness—the mystical reunion of male and female heralded by the returning of the Shekhinah.

Notes

1. According to a midrash, Adam had a wife before Eve, Lilith. Lilith was exiled from Eden, because she wanted to dominate Adam, and instead the more submissive Eve was created. *Talmud* (from the Hebrew root *lamad*, instruct) is a compilation of Jewish law and legend, comprising the Mishnah (traditionally the oral law) and the Gemarah, a commentary on the Mishnah, the "Jerusalem" version completed ca. 400 and the "Babylonian Talmud" ca. 500.

2. The classical period of midrash lasted approximately from 70 CE to 400 CE in ancient Judea, but collections of midrashim were compiled, there and in Babylonia, until the sixteenth century. For information on the history of midrash, as well as on its many-faceted relations to literary studies, see for example Geoffrey Hartman and Sanford Budick, eds., *Midrash and Literature*.

3. Cf. the laws against sexual relations with family members, expressed in the phrase "thou shalt not uncover the nakedness of thy father," etc., in Leviticus 18:6ff.

4. In his essay on Ruth, J. Hillis Miller similarly insists that "there must be at certain crucial points in Old Testament history something approaching incest" (329). Miller draws attention to Boas's ancestress Tamar, who sleeps with her father-in-law Judah in order to continue the line of her dead husband. Both of these near-incestuous relations take place within the framework of the cultural tradition of the levirate marriage (one next of kin marrying a widow to beget progeny in the name of the deceased husband), and together they eventually lead to the birth of King David and in the Christian tradition to that of Jesus.

5. The value given to interpretation in Jewish thinking is signaled by another midrash, quoted by Ostriker, which says that dreams are dependent on their interpretation (109).

6. The translation of this quotation is taken from the T'rumath Tzvi translation of *The Pentateuch*, New York, Judaica Press, 1986. All other Bible quotations appear as in Ostriker's text.

7. The entries on Kabbalah and Shekhinah in the *Encyclopaedia Judaica* may serve as an introduction to these matters.

Works Cited

Genesis Rabbah: The Judaic Commentary to the Book of Genesis—A New American Translation. Edited and translated by Jacob Neusner. 3 vols. Brown Judaic Studies. Atlanta: Scholars Press, 1985. 104–6.

Handelman, Susan. "Jacques Derrida and the Heretic Hermeneutic." In *Displacement: Derrida and After*, edited by Mark Krupnick. Bloomington: Indiana University Press, 1983. 98–132.

Hartman, Geoffrey, and Sanford Budick, eds. *Midrash and Literature*. New Haven: Yale University Press, 1986.

Miller, J. Hillis. "Border Crossings, Translating Theory: Ruth." *Topographies*. Stanford, CA: Stanford University Press, 1995. 316–37.

Neusner, Jacob. *Invitation to Midrash: The Workings of Rabbinic Bible Interpretation*. San Francisco: Harper, 1989.

Ostriker, Alicia Suskin. *The Nakedness of the Fathers: Biblical Visions and Revisions*. New Brunswick, NJ: Rutgers University Press, 1994.

Parfitt, Will. *Kabbala*. Boras: Forum, 1997. Swedish trans. Mikael Hedlund. Originally published in English as *The Elements of the Qabalah*. Shaftesbury, UK: Element Books, 1991.

Stern, David. *Midrash and Theory: Ancient Jewish Exegesis and Contemporary Literary Studies*. Evanston, IL: Northwestern University Press, 1996.

Stern, David. *Parables in Midrash: Narrative and Exegesis in Rabbinic Literature*. Cambridge, MA: Harvard University Press, 1991.

JILL HAMMER

When the Mother Is Dancing
Maternal Theology in the volcano sequence

honor your mother
what if it commanded only that
honor your mother

In section three of "december 1998–january 1999: Ruthless Radi-
ance," the first two months recounted in the twelve-month se-
quence of *the volcano sequence* poems, Alicia Ostriker begins a narra-
tive about a primary relationship that extends throughout the entire
work. She posits an inescapable relationship to the mother—the
repressed, worshipped, despised, rejected, longed-for mother. This
mother is Ostriker's own mother, as well as the mother-chain of
human history, and she is also the divine mother—the Goddess
long repressed by Western society. In returning again and again to
this theme, Ostriker creates not only poetry but theology. Using her
poet's voice as if it is creating sacred text or philosophy, she pains-
takingly feels out a tender (but never naive) vocabulary for birth,
womanhood, suffering, and the human condition. By expressing
her rage, fascination, and dialogue with the mother, Ostriker offers
a radical language for naming mothers and naming God.

Throughout *the volcano sequence*—a book in which few poems
have titles, just as sections of the scroll of the Torah have no titles—
Ostriker invites us into her cosmological imagination. She speaks to
God as a missing lover, as an incomprehensible force, as an absent
father, and as a criminal responsible for the excesses of religion. She
frequently speaks to God as mother, and to her mother as God.
Through this dialogue, Ostriker demands that the male God and his
adherents, as well as all children of mothers, confront this composite
mother-Goddess as an alternate image of the Creator.

In making this radical demand for attention to the power of
women/the feminine, Ostriker uses her Jewish roots. She combines
traditional kabbalah with feminist philosophy, Jewish prayer-

language with ancient goddess stories. Through this amalgam, Ostriker makes clear that she is not rejecting her tradition so much as wrestling with it. In the same way, Ostriker shows us both her love and her pain as a daughter of a human mother—she neither rejects her mother(s) nor uncritically affirms her/them. Through her wrestle, Ostriker offers us a potent new myth about the formation of the human psyche and the spiritual education of the female soul.

the mother's fault

honor your mother
what if it commanded only that
honor your mother

against nature which
bids you flee her
honor while despising

while wrestling free
while avenging
this unasked for

gift of life

~

unasked for disappointing hateful life
it is the mother's fault

we fall from her space into the world
webs of organs helpless

what a pity she does not eat us
and be done with it

rats do
lions do

in dry times

The poem alludes to the biblical command to honor one's parents. Yet instead of the Bible, the poem grounds itself in the image of the devouring mother: the angry ocean-goddess Tiamat in ancient Sumerian myth, the witch in the Grimm stories. Ostriker suggests that these myths arise from our anger at our mothers for giving us "unasked for disappointing hateful life." She is positing not only an origin for our resentment of mothers, but an origin for patriarchy. "Honor while despising // while wrestling free" implies the psychological need to separate from the mother. Yet Ostriker also suggests we have an unconscious wish that she "eat us / and be done with it"—that the mother (human or cosmic) come back and take away the painful reality of life, swallowing us back into the undifferentiated state. An additional source of suffering and rage ensues when the mother fails to re-absorb us into her womb.

Ostriker postulates that to honor the mother is "against nature," inviting us to contemplate all the ways mothers around the world are despised and erased. Monotheistic religion both exalts and despises the mother, "honoring" women and figures such as the Virgin Mary and the matriarchs of Genesis while maintaining power in the hands of men, and depicting creation as primarily, if not entirely, the work of the Father. Though fear of the devouring, all-powerful mother is one of the engines of Western civilization, Ostriker has a prophetic ethical command for us: that we honor the mother in spite of our resentments and in spite of our history. Ostriker demands of us that we consider "honor your mother" as the root of ethics—the need to honor the creator who has birthed you into your suffering, and therefore to cultivate empathy even for what you fear. Ostriker describes this creator as the web of life, the "red thread" that binds all things together and demands our reverence in spite of its fragility:

> the disturbing red thread
> invisible yet warm
> travels between earth and heaven,
>
> vibrates through starless void . . .
>
> does it carry the pulse
> of our prayers
> like a bulge in a snake
>
> dozing, like a stream
> of hungry, bloody hope, do all
> the red threads join
>
> form a web

Ostriker's red thread is simultaneously the red string of Jewish cus-
tom (used in protective amulets), the umbilical cord, and the thread
of existence connecting all being. Ostriker calls it "the disturbing
red thread," for there is nothing comfortable about being connected
to all being. Instead, this connection implies longing and endless
responsibility. In this Ostriker alludes to the snake in the garden of
Eden, the snake that grants the illumination of consciousness, the
gift of sexuality, and the fear of death. The snake recalls Ostriker's
earlier assertion that the mother is guilty for our suffering—just as
God, who creates the snake, is ultimately responsible for the pain of
humanity.

The red thread bestows a life beyond the self, the knowledge of
our connection to one another and to the All. There is no clear
division between creation and deity—the web connects both and
embodies both. Beginning with the distant and longed-for God,
Ostriker ends with the implication that it is the web of relations
that embodies divinity. This assertion is very similar to feminist neo-
pagan claims about the Goddess, such as the pagan theologian Star-
hawk's assertion that "The Goddess does not rule the world. She is
the world. Manifest in each of us, She can be known internally by
every individual, in all her magnificent diversity."[1] Ostriker's image
of the web of being is also similar to the beliefs of classical Jewish
mystics, as when kabbalist Moses Cordovero writes:

Do not say, This is a stone and not God. God forbid! Rather, all
existence is God, and the stone is a thing pervaded by divinity.
(*Shi'ur Qomah* 206b)

Ostriker is particularly careful, though, not to offer us much com-
fort. "Do all the red threads form a web?" implies doubt. Should we
believe in divinity in a world of isolation and brokenness? Ostriker
continues to take up this question in her explorations of the God-
dess as an aging mother in "Mama/Maya":

what I find in the foreground is you
monologist, mistress of futility
seething through cycles of fat and thin
nervously sorting changeless debris
rags, furniture, rotted steaks
killing and saving, more or less at random,
beetles, roaches, flies,

writing illegible puzzles
dead fish crammed in your ceiling

The Goddess Ostriker introduces in her poetry is not a beautiful Goddess. Unlike the father-god Ostriker names as logical and reasonable, she is neither abstract not orderly. In fact, she appears insane. She talks to herself. She cannot decide between dearth and abundance or between death and life. She saves (and kills) everything in her messy ecosystem—her ceiling heaven is full of dead fish.

In this Ostriker is railing not only at the Goddess but also at her own human mother, who failed to present her with a perfect world, and who ended up old and demented and in need of care:

you dare to call me your mother
I who am merely your irresponsible daughter
without shame you exhibit your toothless face
blindness and helplessness
selfishness memory loss
stinking incontinence
whether I wish or not
it is you, isn't it
I must cherish
mama
maya
even if winter sleet assaults the windows
like urine, hisses *too late, too late*
I myself must decide it's not too late

Just as the previous poem addresses Goddess yet alludes to the human mother, this poem addresses the human mother yet alludes to Goddess. The mother is senile, diseased, helpless—all the things human children fear their parents will become. Depicting the almost superhuman strength of will required not to reject this needy and incontinent being, who claims not to be a mother but rather a dependent child, Ostriker tasks herself with the ethical mandate: "I myself must decide it's not too late." Too late for what? To repair the mother-child bond? To be seen and known as a child by a dependent mother who avoids responsibility?

At this point the reader's attention is directed beyond the human mother almost in a whisper: "mama/maya." Maya is the Hindu term for "illusion"—the world of the physical, the world of suffering—the

Goddess, who is embodied in the body/earth. Mama/Maya is the creatrix and also she who abdicates responsibility for creation—in other words, exactly like the human mother. Her sleet assaults the window like urine, as if the Goddess too is incontinent. And it is her burden Ostriker shoulders: "I myself must decide it's not too late." With the incomprehensible Goddess as with the senile mother, Ostriker herself must make the effort to make sense, to derive meaning. Though ideally Goddess should be the one responsible for existence (just as Ostriker's mother ideally should be responsible for her daughter), the human must make the difficult choice to take responsibility for the divine parent and her problematic world.

This is a new take on the Jewish concept of *teshuvah*: turning, return, repentance. For Ostriker, *teshuvah* is not the human sinner turning toward God but an imperfect deity and an imperfect human meeting face to face, as intimates who have disappointed one another. This recalls the well-known Chasidic story in which a Jew tells God on Yom Kippur: "If you will forgive us, we will forgive you!"[2] Yet Ostriker's poem goes even deeper than mutual responsibility. For Ostriker, the human will summons a compassionate God out of the vagaries of nature. The next poem wails:

> mom, reach into
> your barrel of scum-coated blessings.
> find me one.

In three lines, Ostriker depicts the desperation of the human being scavenging for divine/maternal love in the trash heap of a cruel and random world. Even a ruined blessing is better than nothing. Here, Ostriker evokes the anguished plea of Esau, the brother of Jacob, after Jacob steals Esau's blessing: "Have you only one blessing? Bless me too, Father!" (Genesis 27:38). The receiver of the blessing knows the blessing is fatally flawed, but desires even a soiled gesture of love. So Ostriker depicts herself as a child hungry for the affection of a deeply imperfect deity-parent.

you're my mother my sisters my daughters / you're me

A thread or web of being defines Ostriker's understanding of Goddess and of herself. Ostriker identifies not only her own mother, but the generational chain of mothers, as an embodiment of Goddess. In "The Shekhinah as Exile" divinity accompanies the diaspora:

hidden one: when the temple fell
when Jerusalem arose and fell and whenever
we were persecuted and scattered
by the nations,
to follow us in pain in exile
you folded wings patched coats
dragged mattresses pans in peasant carts, lived your life
laboring praying and giving birth, you also
swam across the hard Atlantic
landed in the golden land
they called you greenhorn
you danced in cafes
you went in the factory . . .
put on makeup threw away wigs

This poem is an extrapolation of the Jewish legend, found in rabbinic literature and Jewish mysticism, that the feminine Divine presence—called Shekhinah or "indwelling"—goes into exile with the Jewish people to comfort them in their sorrow.[3] Ostriker uses traditional Jewish imagery to connect to God as female. Yet she also adds something radical: the Shekhinah not only goes with the Jewish people, but is embodied in Jewish women in all their variety: piety and impiety. Embodied in Jewish female lives, Shekhinah patches coats, loads peasant carts, prays, gives birth, becomes an immigrant, throws away her traditional wig. Ostriker tells us near the end of the poem that "you died forever with the sheep / whoever survived, you speak in our tongues" (*volcano* 25), suggesting that the whole Jewish people embodies the Shekhinah—an idea drawn from the kabbalah.[4]

Yet the poem begins "hidden one"—and for Ostriker, even a Goddess revealed in the motherline is still hidden. The forgetting of Goddess across years of monotheist patriarchy can only be undone with difficulty. In "earth: the shekhinah as amnesiac," Ostriker writes:

come on, surely by now you remember who you are
you're my mother my sisters my daughter
you're me

we will have to struggle so hard
to birth you
this time

the brain like a cervix

This poetic image takes the mind out of the realm of the rational, disembodied world of ideas and depicts the human creative function as a birthing process. To this end, Ostriker presents us with a creation narrative entirely focused on the birthing of women. In Genesis, God speaks to create. For Ostriker, creation embodies itself in the bloody birthings of women. She begins this poem-series by telling us that the Sanskrit word for ritual is related to blood—implying that religion itself (as Judy Grahn has suggested)[5] was once formed in response to the bleeding of women's bodies:

a woman squats in the field
wheat stubble pricks her feet
smell of clods billows up

foggy middle of winter
air damp she shivers
she bleeds it helps the birth

of whatever means to be born

A prayer recited each morning in Jewish liturgy reads: "blessed is the one who spoke, and the world came into being." Ostriker juxtaposes this image of speaker-as-creator to an ancient fertilization ritual dependent on menstrual blood. "ten thousand years later,"

a woman writhes on a straw mat they can't hold her
digs nails into palms against the contractions . . .

she lashes out at the midwives
why does nobody push the sun forward

Like Abraham Joshua Heschel,[6] Ostriker is portraying the pathos of God—yet not only in relational terms, but in physical terms. In the next poem Ostriker walks us through a modern hospital birth with its tubes and rubber pads, and then "a woman // sun warm on her back / . . . is rocking back / and forth now":

everyone who sees her laughs

hold on hold on push
now is the time
somebody catch the child

This is a timeless birth, and Ostriker finally lets us feel its joy, the intense miracle of the production of life. In four birthing poems, Ostriker has fused for us the image of our mothers with the image of Goddess bleeding, writhing, laughing. In images made out of words, Ostriker reverses for us the biblical image of God speaking the world into creation, and substitutes an archetypal birth that happens again and again throughout the generations, infinitely varied yet all part of one umbilical chain of life: "somebody catch the child" reminds us that ultimately the life Goddess joyfully produces is in our hands.

In speaking of Goddess, Ostriker revalues the Jewish notion of exile and redemption to include the exile and redemption of women. For Ostriker, the exile of women includes their inability to speak of the Goddess. Silenced by patriarchy, they carry the Goddess within, but are unable to express her in words.

our mothers tremble vibrate
hesitate at the edge of speech . . .

our mothers helpless to tell us
She whom you seek sacrificed
her place before the throne

dived into the atomic structure
of matter and hides there
hair wings streaming

womb compassionate pitiless
eyes seeing to the ends of the universe
in which life struggles and delights in life . . .

they cannot say *seek me*
they teach us cooking clothing craftiness
they tell us their own stories of power and shame

and even if it is she who speaks through their mouths
and has crawled through ten thousand wombs until this day
we cannot listen

their words fall like spilled face powder

Here, Ostriker grants us a full picture of her mother deity: winged, compassionate, and pitiless, embodying the entire chain of being and nonbeing. The mothers are all of these things, yet they do not know it.

raise the sparks

In another poem connected to memory and repression, Ostriker imagines the subconscious as a *geniza*, a hidden repository of sacred texts. In this secret place, the terebinth grove of the goddess has been hidden: "her terebinth   grove misremembered." In Hebrew the terebinth is *elah*, a word for Goddess, and was considered a sacred tree. Yet the *geniza* waits for anyone who is able to find it: "the mind can't / throw anything holy away / let it stay let it be she   let it wait." The image of the Goddess waits in human consciousness to arise again, as all repressed truths inevitably arise. Elsewhere Ostriker writes:

all poetry is, you say,

> *an attempt*
> *to name the disappearance*
> *that got in the way . . . —*

it's the goddess, let's face it—
when they chopped her groves down
nailed her shrines shut
forgot the words to her songs

when she stalked back to myth
we lost something worth having
the men did it but the women
cooperated as usual . . .

we need to blame someone
we scream at our mothers

where is she? what have you
done with her?

"We lost something worth having," the poet tells us, reversing centuries of monotheistic certainty that the pagan/feminine past was a good thing to discard. Now the daughters want the Goddess back—they want their mothers to admit—or embody—the buried truth.

Ostriker sometimes depicts the arising of repressed truth as the birth of the female out of the male. As in her story "Intensive Care" in *The Nakedness of the Fathers*, Ostriker depicts the rebirth of the Goddess as a birth from the Father. The patriarchal God who swallowed the Goddess must now deliver her out of the depths of himself and into the world: "your labor pains persist indefinite exacerbate. . . ."

oh god, yours and ours, how they hurt so . . .
she so buried so erased so unlawful so forgot so swallowed . . .
meanwhile in the text she kicks watch that . . .

This is the feminist fantasy of men giving birth, but with a productive twist. The being called God the Father, who has never really been father or mother but both or neither, must now bring forth a "uterine self," a maternal deity-form. This uterine self has always existed within God the Father, somewhere under the surface, erupting and kicking, showing her presence in the biblical text and throughout history. Ostriker compares the forgotten, erased Goddess to the grandmother in Little Red Riding Hood, who emerges alive and whole when the woodcutter opens the belly of the wolf. The wolf dies in this process, as indeed might the patriarchal god. Ostriker defines this part of her poetic work as an effort "to speak the spoken unspeakable," which is a kind of midwifery. She wants to aid in pulling out the swallowed Goddess from the womb/tomb of Western religion.

Ostriker's vision of the rebirth of the Goddess out of the body of the God who swallowed her can be defined as messianic. Messianism is a strain that has existed in Judaism from its earliest roots: from Isaiah's vine and fig tree, to the Talmud's vision of a beggar Messiah on the streets of Rome, to the Lurianic hope of a repaired cosmos (Isaiah 36:16).[7] In the messianic belief system of Jewish mystics, the brokenness of the universe can be ultimately made whole through crucial healing or mending events, events that occur because of human action. Ostriker sees herself as part of this feminist messianic activity. Yet Ostriker's messianism is not romantic, nor is it supernatural. In Ostriker's vision, we cease to idealize God as a perfect, dispassionate, theoretically and platonically male being detached from a perversely damaged world. Instead, we learn to see holiness in the failing, ruined, fat and scrawny bodies of our mothers. When we can honor our origins in their true, beautiful, and ugly reality, we will be able to achieve true appreciation and empathy for our own beautiful and ugly lives.

> when she comes it will not be from heaven, it will be up from the cunts and breasts
>
> it will be from our insane sad fecund obscure mothers
>
> it will be from our fat scrawny pious wild ancestresses their claws
>
> their fur and their rags (*the volcano sequence*)

My Mother, My Queen

Feminists from Western spiritual traditions long have attempted to relate the God of the Bible to the Goddess/goddesses of the ancient world. For some, such as Sue Monk Kidd, this is a process of uneasy rapprochement, bringing together Christian imagery with goddess imagery, while for others, such as Carol Christ, this is a process of eventual rejection of the biblical god in favor of a worldview shaped by the goddesses.[8] The question of how the Goddess is to be integrated into traditions that have long repressed her remains open.

Jewish feminists too have struggled with the question of how to integrate a female face of God. Some Jewish feminists, such as Leah Novick, use the "legitimate" mystical and rabbinic term *Shekhinah* when talking about the divine feminine.[9] Others, such as Lynn Gottlieb, use the term *Shekhinah* but also the imagery of Asherah, Anat, and Tiamat—Near Eastern goddesses—in creating new names for God.[10] Still others, such as Marcia Falk, invent Hebrew, grammatically feminine language that is nonpersonal: fountain of life, source of blessing.[11] Feminist scholars such as Max Dashu research ancient Near Eastern goddesses to show how their presence was repressed (or reconstituted) by the Bible and/or later religious authorities.[12] Other Jewish women, such as Starhawk (born Miriam Simos), have turned from Jewish tradition to Goddess religion.[13]

In her poems in *the volcano sequence*, Ostriker offers us a complex relationship between God and Goddess, one that is imagistic and intertextual. Ostriker neither rejects her Jewish tradition nor accepts its boundaries. Her juxtapositions of goddess-language and monotheistic language engage the divine as mysterious, unpredictable, ever-present, and yet unnameable—and continue to engage the mother as a fundamental source of spiritual experience.

> when her hands cup her breasts
> she enjoys her sweet strength
> sap ascends the oak
>
> dancing she causes
> the young to dance
> and to kiss
>
> she may carry a weapon
> a knife a gun a razor
> she may wear a belt of skulls . . .
>
> when she discharges her anger in laughter
> white lightning illuminates the horizon
> from pole to pole
>
> often she lays her hand over her eyes
> like a secretary leaving
> an office building at evening
>
> cradling that infant boy
> sitting him on her lap
> smoothing the folds of her dress: this means pity
>
> arms crossed: this means judgment

In this poem, Ostriker takes us on a whirlwind tour of potential Goddess language. She delves into ancient Near Eastern iconography in which small pottery statues cup their breasts, and also Hindu imagery where the goddess Kali dances with skulls on her belt. The terrifying laughing Goddess is an image of Aphrodite.[14] Ostriker reminds us of both Isis and the Virgin Mary "cradling that infant boy."[15] Yet she also presents a surprising contemporary image: "a secretary leaving / an office building at evening." Through this contemporary "breaking" of ancient metaphors for deity, she reminds us that we draw images for God from our own lives.

Finally, Ostriker returns to her own tradition. In the Talmudic understanding of God, and later in the mystical understanding, God has two major aspects, mercy and judgment (Cf. Exodus 34:6–7, Genesis Rabbah 12:15). God is even depicted on Yom Kippur praying "May my mercy overcome my judgment."[16] In her poem, Ostriker invites us to consider the Goddess as source of compassion and severity: when she is cradling a child, she is the source of pity and love; when her arms are folded, she is the stern judge. Of course, Ostriker is reminding us of how we humans got the image of mercy and judgment to begin with: the mother who hugs and holds us and also punishes and says "no."

> and in the whiteness a speck
> but god was not in the speck
> then a soft wind
> but god was not in the wind
> then a breast and a great hand

Here Ostriker is interpreting a famous biblical text from Kings (I Kings 19:11–13). The prophet Elijah comes out of his cave and stands on the mountain. He sees a fire, but God is not in the fire. He sees an earthquake, but God is not in the earthquake. He sees a wind, but God is not in the wind. God appears to be in the still, small voice that comes after these elemental forces. The text is a strong statement of God's disembodiment: God does not exist in nature but apart from it.

Ostriker's poem does not take place on a mountain. It takes place in a birthing room. The whiteness is the blinding light the infant sees. The speck in the whiteness is the approach of the mother, midwife, father—the first object (or it could also be the aureole of the nipple). The soft wind is the mother's breath. And the breast and the great hand is the first embrace, the first suckling.

Ostriker turns the experience of the prophet into the experience of the birthed child, and turns the God of the still small voice into the Goddess of the breast and the great hand. In so doing, the poet strengthens her assertion that our ideas about God come from our early experiences with the mother. Yet Ostriker is also alluding to the God-name El Shaddai, which can mean "God of breasts."[17] She is hinting at a rabbinic midrash that describes the study of Torah as being like nursing from God: "Just as a suckling child finds fresh flavor each time the child nurses at the breasts, so too will one who pores over the teachings of the Torah."[18] Ostriker is recycling tradition even as she undermines it. Her relationship to Torah is one of loyalty as well as rebellion.

> first dream I remember
> maybe I was three
> wearing a little coat
> you were pushing a baby carriage
> down the block away from me
> you were running
> my mother my queen
> I was trying to catch you

In this moving poem, Ostriker describes her childhood dream of losing her mother, using liturgical terms. "My mother my queen" strongly echoes the Jewish prayer-phrase "our father our king," repeated over and over again during the High Holidays. Through the use of this phrase, Ostriker not only reverses God's gender, but also provides the reader with a poignant understanding of what it means to seek God: it is to seek the lost parent, the abandoning caretaker. The longing for God is visceral, primal, connected to our earliest needs and terrors.

The "little coat" the child wears in the poem is also a reference to biblical text. In the book of Samuel, Hannah gives her son Samuel at a very early age to be a servant in the shrine at Shiloh. She does this in fulfillment of a vow that if God would grant her a son, she would give him up to serve God. Every year, at the season of pilgrimage, Hannah brings Samuel a little coat she makes (I Samuel 1–2). The "little coat" is a symbol of maternal love and also maternal abandonment: the very themes Ostriker points to in trying to understand her relationship with God.

Here, Ostriker asserts, as she asserts again and again throughout *the volcano sequence*, that the relationship to God is subject to personal myth, and cannot be contained by a dictated theology. This is one of the ways Ostriker reconciles tradition with iconoclasm—by asserting her own language, resonant with the Bible and Jewish lore yet deeply affected by her childhood, her feminism, her poetry, and her quest for the truth. Ostriker's demand for attention to the mother is not a new orthodoxy but an invitation to explore the inner landscape without fear or preconception.

you created this caldera now full of windmills
we finish our lunch of olive and feta, we bike the flat dirt roads

mountain crests ringing the irrigated land like a signature
of your name—a bluegray zero

one of your many fists probably a meteor did this
all is verdant fertile now in rows

where earth loosens her dress
more of your signs

Ostriker's goddess is always mistress of both life and death: as here where she is the verdant fertility of the land and also the many-fisted mother of meteors. In this poem, the goddess is clearly Nature herself—yet the "bluegray zero" is very similar to a kabbalistic term for the transcendent, hidden deity: *Ayin* or nothingness. *Ayin* is the name of the Divine before creation, the name of the part of God that is completely separate from physicality and to which humans have almost no access.[19] This part of God exists prior to the creation of masculine and feminine and prior to anything that could be called substance. The caldera of the meteor, the empty space created by the fist of the Goddess, reminds Ostriker of the platonic, ideal god called "nothing."

Ultimately Ostriker wants to see beyond gender to the infinitely personal connection with the ultimate. Because she refuses a duality of God and Goddess, Ostriker stands somewhere between the apologists and the rejectionists. Ostriker is carrying on the legacy of Jewish mystics and of contemporary feminists at the same time.

Conclusion: Somebody Catch the Child

While Ostriker's theology is on view in much of her written work, her collection *the volcano sequence* delves into it most deeply and personally. She foregrounds her own need, her own passion, demonstrating that our relationships with God (like our relationships with mothers) are subjective and need-based. Through her own vulnerability and ruthless honesty, Ostriker offers the opportunity for us to radically change our relationship to our mothers—our biological and social mothers, our tribal mothers, our divine mother(s). Indeed, she calls us to smash the boundaries society has built between things female and things divine. Ostriker draws forth the hidden—the divinity of the mother, buried in her psyche and in the psyche of every human being. For the duration of the volume, Ostriker acts as a poet and midwife of the Goddess.

Ostriker's encounter with the mother is theological, but hers is not a theology that can be accused of dogma or of narcissism. Ostriker's poetic vision demands that we encounter the world with empathy, with hope, without denial, without controlling others. She summons us to recognize "the claw of the Shekhinah" and "her / dark smile"—the violence within us, which is also part of the Goddess's world (*volcano* 109). Much earlier in *the volcano sequence*, she honors both beauty and human compassion:

> I have come to worship reflections of traveling cumuli in
> architectural glass
> and I have come to adore the khaki blankets of homeless men . . .
> I have come in humility to beg and scratch in the dust
> of your mass graves until you rise up . . .
>
> until the death of the word "until"
> I don't want you to be proven scientifically, I want you to appear
> to me and to all peoples in your true form
> of ruthless radiance

We are the witnesses to the presence of the Goddess within all people and all things. If we are the ones who must "catch the child" as the mother/goddess gives birth, then we are the hands and voices needed to care for the world. Ostriker's maternal deity provides us with the ground of life (and perhaps even a mother's love), but with no escape from the work of redemption.

Notes

1. Starhawk, *The Spiral Dance* (New York: Harper and Row, 1989), 23.

2. This story is told of Rabbi Levi Yitzchak of Berdichev and a tailor; cf. Alan M. Dershowitz, *The Genesis of Justice: Ten Stories of Biblical Injustice that Led to the Ten Commandments and Morality and Law* (New York: Warner Books, 2000), chapter 4.

3. Leah Novick, *On the Wings of Shekhinah: Rediscovering Judaism's Divine Feminine* (Wheaton, IL: Quest Books, 2008), 59–68.

4. See Zohar III, 93a; Barry Holtz, *Back to the Sources: Reading the Classical Jewish Texts* (New York: Simon and Schuster, 1984), 336–38.

5. Judy Grahn, *Blood, Bread, and Roses: How Menstruation Created the World* (Boston: Beacon Press, 1994).

6. Cf. A. J. Heschel, *God in Search of Man: A Philosophy of Judaism* (New York: Farrar, Strauss, and Cudahy, 1955).

7. See also Babylonian Talmud, Sanhedrin 98a; Gershom Scholem, *Kabbalah* (New York: Meridian, 1978), 128–43, 165–67.

8. Sue Monk Kidd, *Dance of the Dissident Daughter: A Woman's Journey from the Christian Tradition to the Sacred Feminine* (San Francisco: HarperSanFrancisco, 1996); Carol Christ, *Rebirth of the Goddess: Finding Meaning in Feminist Spirituality* (New York: Routledge, 1998); Carol Christ, *Laughter of Aphrodite: Reflections on a Journey to the Goddess* (New York: HarperCollins, 1988).

9. Leah Novick, "Encountering the Shechinah, The Jewish Goddess," in *The Goddess Re-Awakening: The Feminine Principle Today*, ed. Shirley Nicholson (Wheaton, IL: Theosophical Publishing House, 1983), 204–14; Leah Novick, *On the Wings of Shekhinah: Rediscovering Judaism's Divine Feminine* (Wheaton, IL: Quest Books, 2008).

10. Lynn Gottlieb, *She Who Dwells Within: A Feminist Vision of a Renewed Judaism* (San Francisco: HarperSanFrancisco, 1995).

11. Marcia Falk. *The Book of Blessings: New Jewish Prayers for Daily Life, the Sabbath, and the New Moon* (Boston: Beacon Press, 1999).

12. Max Dashu, "Khokhmah and Sophia," in *Streams of Wisdom* (The Oppressed Histories Archive, 2000), chap. 3, available at http://www.adishakti.org/_/khokhmah_and_sophia_by_max_dashu.htm

13. Starhawk, *The Pagan Book of Living and Dying: Practical Rituals, Prayers, Blessings and Meditations on Crossing Over* (New York: HarperOne, 1997), introduction.

14. Theocritus, *Idyll 1*.

15. The ancient Egyptian goddess Isis is depicted holding her son Horus, in a similar vein to the images of the Virgin holding the child Jesus.

16. Babylonian Talmud, Berachot 7a.

17. Harriet Lutzky, "Shaday as a Goddess Epithet," in *Vetus Testamentum* 48 (1998): 15–46. For popular feminist commentary on this etymology, see Aurora Mendelson, "Nursing in Shul," in *Lilith Magazine* (Fall 2009), 27–28, and Susan Schnur in conversation with Susan Weidman Schneider, "What's This about God Being Female? With Breasts and All? How'd This Happen?" in *Lilith Magazine* (Fall 2009): 29.

18. Rashi on Ecclesiastes 1:9.

19. cf. Daniel C. Matt, "Ayin: The Concept of Nothingness in Jewish Mysticism," in *Essential Papers in Kabbalah*, ed. Lawrence Fine (New York: New York University Press, 1994), 43–47.

RICHARD TAYSON

the volcano sequence as Fragmentary, Postmodern, (and Yes, Feminist) Text

the volcano sequence is a contemporary epic, the fragmentation of which is rendered by the book's multiple speakers and by the experimental forms in which Alicia Suskin Ostriker embeds them. She asserts three speakers contextualized by their fragmented worlds: the primary speaker, whom I name, in deference to her own fragmented nature, the voice of the daughter/wife/mother-of-tensile-strength who at times may assume the poet's perspective; an Overlord voice; and the voice, filtered through the primary speaker, of a female version of the psalmist David. The turbulent forms in which these voices erupt are expressive of another voice, albeit one unspoken: that of female Hebrew scholar Bruriah, whose divestment of speech by her second-century CE culture is countered by the fiercely idiosyncratic and architectural forms Ostriker employs in the creation of *volcano*'s world. Though Bruriah is not remembered until the seventh section of the text, "turn and return," Ostriker's deployment of non sequiturs, abrupt transitions, and run-on formulations fosters a series of positive incoherences in which fractured vocalization is the only form appropriate to match the extremity of Bruriah's rage. If Bruriah, cognizant that women in all corners of the globe had been subjected to twenty centuries of mistreatment great and small, suddenly had been telescoped into the twenty-first century, her speech might take the nonlinear form of Ostriker's *volcano*.

Though reading *the volcano sequence* as a quest narrative, as Adrian Oktenberg does in her *Women's Review of Books* essay, "Incandescent Clarity," provides a clear, linear structure, approaching *volcano* as a problem text of Barthesian fragmentation inclines Ostriker's work toward a process in which fractured and disjunctive experiences coalesce within the space of the reader's active mind. Even with female heroes at its core, *volcano* is not a recycled trajectory that spans the distance between the binary of innocence and experience. With its nine sections and 119 pages of intersecting fragments

89

whose partiality strips omniscient narration of its braggadocio and offers multiple counter-voices that obscure the dependability of linear narration, *volcano* allows Ostriker to make her most important contribution to contemporary American poetics: her joining of fragmented experimental forms with the polyvocality of multiple first-person speakers. In a text that defies acceptable behavior, Ostriker manages to maintain the conviction of first-person perspectives within the ever-shifting formal concerns of a Barthes-inflected landscape of incommensurability and radical fragmentation.

A book of photographs of a Greek island and a disembodied voice enabled this self-described "third-generation atheist socialist Jew" to overcome a three-year bout of writer's block (Adams, "Interview"). The disembodied voice, which led Ostriker to a new process of writing, resulted in a pact: "If you agree to keep arriving," she said to the poems, "I agree not to tell you what to say." And so began the collaboration, which led to the cryptic opening of "volcano," the first of five sections comprising Part I, "ruthless radiance":

> Let me speak it to you in a whisper
> I am like a volcano
> that has blown itself
> out of the water

From the start, Ostriker's use of pronouns leads us to consider the first method by which *volcano* inaugurates itself as fragmentary text: who is speaking, and to whom? The speaker here may be the voice of inspiration, but also may be the voice of the God of the book of Genesis taking possession of physical forms (in the next stanza we find "my long stony curve / my melancholiac cliffs"). As also may be the case in the fragment from Part II titled "desert" in which that landscape berates "they who were so in need of fire," this may be the volcano itself speaking. A fourth possibility is that the voice of the book's primary speaker, the daughter/wife/mother-of-tensile-strength, is proffering in internal monologue form ruminations concerning the world around her and her place in it.

As this primary speaker relays the poem as interconnecting breath, these initial utterances become emblematic of the woman who, as she looks out to the external world and into her interior self, will describe, in fragmented form, both her sympathy for and derision of human error, her honoring of past women silenced by their cultures, and her anger at the injustices abundantly evident in the contemporary world. Though we may attempt to determine which of these speakers may be most relevant in imparting "Let me speak it to you in a whisper," one of the salient aspects of *volcano* is that no such cleaving is necessary: these voices are enfolded, one upon the other, in a rich overlay of subtly positive confusion in which no distinct, ever-fixed narrative voice acts as an auditory aperture through which the poems' perspectives may be heard. In contrast to the distinct speakers of Louise Glück's *The Wild Iris* (1992), Ostriker's speakers are in rich states of superimposition in which narrative voice is splintered into multiples, sometimes within the bounds of single lines. The reader gets to choose among possible speakers: a singular voice, dual (and often dueling) voices, or a choral configuration of orators.

Equally rich with possibility is the opening line's "you." Though the second-person address implicates the reader, this pronoun also may refer to God, to whom the speaker registers her objection about his lackluster concern for his creation, his absence from the physical world. Another possibility is that she is speaking to her mother, who, in the frailty of dying (another form of pending absence), is central to the book as a whole. From its opening lines, the reader encounters two of the primary challenges in reading *volcano*: who is speaking at any given time, and who is the shifting "you" to whom the poems are addressed with such revelatory intimacy?

With the intentional (and productive) confusion of these opening lines, the poem's form generates its own disequilibrium of the fragmentary context in which Ostriker's multiple points of vocalization cohere. Resplendent with quick movement resulting, in part, from Ostriker's minimal use of punctuation, the form creates a sort of swoon, movement above and below and sideways in a rush that ends, sudden as the return of an ocean-roiled swimmer to terra firma, with "you remember." With but a single comma this initial fragment leads readers through the Aegean world of whisper, volcano, "old hard / exoskeleton," gawking tourists, tidal wave, myth, the imagining of "a green good world" (3). This "you"—the reader? the volcano speaking to the writer? the writer addressing God? God addressing the daughter/wife/mother-of-tensile-strength?—is as richly obscure as the voice speaking the poem.

Obscurity of the speech act is of central concern, and it receives direct treatment in the book's first brief prose poem, "descent": "Whoever is speaking or will speak in these pages, I welcome you.

Let me be your vehicle. Let me be the mouth of your tunnel. Or the split in the earth." Sounding dangerously close, for an atheist, to prayer, "mouth" implies being of service to an Overlord spirit, and thus attracts the positive valence of conductivity, of vehicular transmission. "[S]plit," on the other hand, imparts a decidedly different form of speech act: a sacrifice indicative of violence done to the self in response to the crushing demands of a creator. Divisible perspectives of self, sometimes produced by contrasting linguistic terms, drive the book's voices, fracture them into specula refracting light back from the radiant Source and speaking in fragments. Imperfection is a given, and contrary to the suggestion in some sentimental interpretations of Whitman's "I am large, I contain multitudes," the fact of multiplicity is not always comforting. Rather, in its dizzying array of potentialities, the selves found in *volcano* are corrective to the simplistic (and always partial) binary constructs of female/male, Jew/Gentile, black/white, gay/straight. The first-person self in *volcano* is fluid and, as such, asserts a self-correcting ontological accuracy. The notion of Whitmanian multitudes imparts a sense of proliferating states of being within the writerly (and readerly) self, a decentering, pluralistic, and pluralizing appropriation of self aligned with the fragmentary nature of human personality, which is to say the multitudinous qualities in which personality manifests. *volcano* implies that comfortably unified selves do not exist—at least not in any real way. Coherence of self is, in an interpretation of Barthes's "distorting order," cozy fantasy.

The vocal fracturing that occurs in the book's opening continues in the second poem fragment in which the voice of daughter/wife/mother-of-tensile-strength responds to "A woman [who] looked at my poem" and asked, "What makes you like a volcano?" The speaker responds by indicating that "something terrible happens," followed by a portrayal of violent images in which "the magma / coughs out // hot beauty / thick and magnificent rage." Yet behind this "hot beauty" lie little Greek isles scattered across the scintillating blue, and the speaker states, perhaps with an irony that renders multiple meanings possible, "so what if afterward // everything is dead." Then in the following fragment, this voice, splitting off into the daughter portion of her tripartite form, depicts her child self as "an island." What is striking is the minimal part innocence plays in her early self, for her childlike joy is quickly reconfigured within a matrix of anger that "destroy[s] all / in its path / righteously // roaring." In a reference perhaps to Susan Griffin's *Woman and Nature: The Roaring Inside Her* (1978) and/or to Matthew Arnold's "long withdrawing roar," Ostriker quotes in the "Creation" chapter of her celebrated *The Nakedness of the Fathers: Biblical Visions and Revisions* (1994), that conflation of innocence with destruction dismantles any vestige of an innocence/experience simplistic binary. As we are then taken back to the "amniotic worm" of fertilization, violence prevails within the context of "flags and bombs bursting" in ironic American glory (especially when noted beside the "bombs [that] fall / like vapor" into "thin air" over Kosovo in Part IV, "covenant"), and the daughter/wife/mother-of-tensile-strength asserts, in the final line of the sixth fragment of Part I, "doomed either way, dear God." Atlantis or no Atlantis, tsunami or lack thereof, the child is catapulted toward her eventual death, with mud, tears, money, bombs, honey, love, dislocation, images of homelessness, greed, and some beauty along the way.

Here and elsewhere, God watches (or not), leading the mother-of-tensile-strength speaker in section two of Part I, "the unmasking," to "rave like Jonah" and indict him in quintessentially American contexts, "beery ballparks," "your hysterical stock exchanges," and "your hypocritical congresses," all disguises for worldly embodiments of God's eminence. Though the second-person pronoun seems to implicate those who created and now populate the stadiums, Wall Street, and Washington, the mother's vitriol is aimed first and foremost at God, as the poem's epigraph by Abraham Joshua Heschel, implies: "I have come to sow the seed of light in the world / To unmask the God who disguises Himself as world." Thus the "dear God" that ends the previous section becomes a linguistic conduit through which the mother-of-tensile-strength shifts tone and registers her disappointment (verging on disdain) for the terrible physical forms of suffering that reflect God's ruthlessness, here abundantly radiant. True to the brawniness of her personality, she ends the section with a demand: "I want you to appear / to me and to all peoples in your true form / of ruthless radiance." This petition opens the way for the book's exchanges, sometimes in Socratic form, Overlord and underling exchanges between the daughter/wife/mother and also with the God she holds in contempt, not only for global suffering but for being an absentee landlord in a world where pain is as commonplace as ocean tides.

A central paradox of *volcano* is that even though the Overlord maintains presence, however distant and unapproachable, via spoken language, at numerous junctures in the text the wife speaker berates him for being absent. There exists a discrepancy between a God whom the speaker admonishes for his absence, and the God whose speech acts form part of *volcano's* utterances. "so where in hell / are you now," the wife asks at the end of "ruthless radiance." "you can tell I'm lonely." Though this may be directed at a husband, it may also be levied at God (or, perhaps, both, in another example of Ostriker's ability to offer simultaneous meanings). In a poem titled "waste" from the next part, "the red thread," this speaker accuses God of being "the absent mathematician" who is "behind it all." Even as the Overlord speaks at various points, the primary speaker—often in the wife portion of her tripartite form—continues to insist on his absence. "where are you damn you," she implores as late as the seventh section, "turn and return," "beloved where are you." It appears that what the speaker here desires is God's demonstrable presence, the irrefutability of visible, as opposed to vocal, appearance. Verbal locutions, it seems, will not suffice (an irony since the book is, of course, formed wholly of language). Not only will the Overlord refuse visible embodiment, the speaker is understandably resentful that when the Overlord "appears" in verbal form, rather than granting consolation to humanity mired in the "dried blood in the newsprint" (8) of worldly suffering, the Overlord is more concerned with alleviating his own discomfort. "*I tried to invent new forms of holiness / to console myself*," he says to the shock of both the wife speaker and, probably, the reader who expects compassion (23). To find in this Overlord utterance—the first in the book—a reference to both his skill of invention and his selfish attitude is, to put it mildly, disheartening.

It only gets worse, for in this section titled "dialogue," though the daughter/wife/mother-of-tensile-strength has finally heard God's voice, not only is that voice lacking concern for her, it also comes to insult her. After exhibiting self-gratifying tendencies, he refers to "*the event at the mountain*" where he says he "*put before you / life and death therefore / choose life.*" But his creation, alas, did not choose life, and now God has nothing (here, at least) but chastising words:

> but look at you
> look at the stiffness of your neck
> look at the desire of your heart
> to wreck everything
>
> with your harlotry

Noteworthy here is that, as indicated by the word "harlotry," the Overlord degrades the inquisitor who has demonstrated bravery and daring (not to mention ever-eroding patience) by approaching him. In an effort to control her, he deploys language to humiliate her into submission. By noting "*the desire of your heart / to wreck everything*," the Overlord voice lays claim to the belief—repeated by those in power in nearly every culture known to woman—that she will manipulate the opposite sex, thereby causing the disintegration of the social order. Even as reproduction was of inestimable value to the continuation of early human civilization, the Overlord maintains that the female body has the power to "*wreck everything*"— social class, governance, trade economies. Though "menstrual blood" will not be mentioned until Part III's "deaths, transfigurations," it, along with the pregnancy cycle, is a coded sign of what is ungovernable about female nature. Overlord humiliation is a bid for female submission.

The wife, however, isn't buying it and takes the only sensible action available for the unjustly accused: defensive argumentation. "I am named *k'dsha*, harlot, whore, abomination," she reasons in the face of his grand paradox, "while you are named *kaddosh*, holy, separate or apart." Upon birth, girls are nominated as unclean sources of potential attraction for the opposite gender, while boys, capable of obfuscation of their sexual selves due to the fact of their lack of menses, are "holy, separate or apart." In the eyes of the Overlord and the society that functions to maintain the dogmatic structure of his sanctity, femininity is by definition an "abomination," while masculinity, oddly enough noted for its "logic and reason," is prized for its ability to divide (and, it may be assumed, conquer). This double standard is at the core of both the rage the wife expresses here and elsewhere to the Overlord, and the perverse logic by which the Overlord maintains his self-centered status of verbal presence.

In addition to employing the language of the bully, the voice of Overlord also slips easily into riddle, though to be fair, the Overlord has the capacity to evince empathy, once declaring to the daughter/ wife/mother "*your pain is mine*" and "*when the least portion of you suffers I curl / wincing into myself like a sea urchin*." Not only his use of self-serving language creates distrust and a lack of intimacy between him and his female charge, but also his riddles, often with human shortcoming as their punch lines, have the power to annoy, as in Part IV, "covenant":

the spot of black paint
in the gallon of white
makes it whiter

so the evil impulse
is part of you
for a reason

"[W]hat reason," inquires the primary speaker, to which the Overlord responds, "*greater wilder holiness.*" Reason is not here reasonable. Suffering, he seems to say, cleanses the palate, and a little breakage gives us something to fix. Is it any wonder that fragmentation takes forceful shape in Ostriker's *volcano*, not only in the form of a recognition that singularity of cohesive personality is exemplary of Barthes's "distorting order," but also in the form of separation: distance from God and isolation from one's fellows, and even oneself?

After God attempts in his first verbal expression to console himself by berating his female creation, Ostriker's wife, as if at the end of her rope and in need of an alternative to an Overlord who manifests verbally as either hard-hearted judgment or hijinks riddle, posits an alternative, an Overlord substitute. "you do not speak to us / or you speak to us in riddles," she will soon protest, thus giving reason for her to seek God's female emanation, the shekhinah. The shekhinah is a "hidden one," "part . . . wounds / part . . . words," the female spirit who "follow[s] us in pain in exile" and who manifests not in the plenitude of airy vocalization, but in objects, places, and events that matter to the human struggle to survive: "patched coats," "peasant carts," cafes, factories, "Hester Street," wigs, and of course "laboring praying and giving birth." No pie-in-the-sky Overlord here, and the fact of the shekhinah's arrival amid the earthly locations of human experience opens a way for the daughter speaker to solicit aid. "say what we are / say what we are to do," she implores in an act that both returns us to the daughter/wife/mother-of-tensile-strength speaker's imperative that the Overlord allow her to "be the mouth of your tunnel" and "the split in the earth," as well as moving her (and us) toward the figuration of alternative female voices that will displace the reluctant, riddled, and abusive speech of the Overlord.

The shekhinah—and, soon, the figure of Bruriah—becomes the force by which the primary speaker aligns fragments, pieces together what is broken. But the process is daunting, which the daughter/ wife/mother-of-tensile-strength admits. "when I try to look into my soul," she allows, "something always interrupts . . . Is it that mother will be angry // that the universe will forget me / that the soul will be empty / or like a broken jar." Her uncertainty is punctuated by the Overlord voice, which states, cryptically, "the best soul is the most empty / the most broken." Not quite what the speaker needs to hear in the post-9/11 vale of soul making, but fragmentation promises—however distant the prospect—wholeness, a remaking of the shards. "we destroy we break we are broken," she laments, which represents a negative valence of the fragmentary poetics that underlie Ostriker's *volcano*, and she desires alternative voices that have a chance, however slight, of putting together the pieces. Part of that effort entails her recognition concerning who the shekhinah is: "you're my mother my sisters my daughter / you're me // we will have to struggle so hard / to birth you." The birth of the shekhinah is also the symbolic rebirth of the daughter/wife/mother-of-tensile-strength, and that requires much more than simply gathering one's heritage, especially since that heritage has been erased, either partially or wholly. Self-discovery is an act of excavation, especially when one is searching for one's female progenitors. Never taking no for an answer, the primary speaker digs, both within and without, until she encounters another voice to add to her arsenal: that of the psalmist David, in female form.

Six poems in *volcano*, each with "psalm" in its title, are rendered in the mode (or, perhaps more accurately, the antimode) of a female David. Though the Anti-David/wife speaker seeks an Overlord alternative in the form of the female emanation of the shekhinah, that quest is not fully realized. Though she admits to a shekhinah spirit, she falls back to the default of Overlord's linguistic presence. Yet with the Bruriah inflection in *volcano*'s experimentation with consistently bold forms, the poem functions not only as linguistic vessel, but as proposition, confrontation, and as alternative worldview. "I have suffered through silence, have spoken only when spoke to, have been polite and respectful of the eminence of God's grace," the form seems to say, "and now I've had it up to my ass with sedate. I will now let loose what has been for centuries inside me." What she lets loose are 119 pages of uncommonly original, late-twentieth-century poetry, rife with non sequiturs, run-ons, abrupt transitions, and experimental linear placement—all appropriate expressions of how Bruriah, female scholar tricked, silenced, and left behind without even the dignity of a gravestone, might speak if she were to return, knowledge intact, to the contemporary world. If Bruriah had known, when she had access to scholarly texts and instruments to register her opinions in codified, linguistic form, what was to transpire in terms of her own pending humiliation, if she had watched as centuries passed and women remained at the mercy of male counterparts (arranged marriages, is this a joke? lack of women's free movement in some parts of the world, is this a joke? no female president in over 225 years of American life, is this a joke?), her words might have taken the shape of Ostriker's *volcano*. Correlative to Bruriah's response to what she endured eighteen centuries ago, Ostriker's radically experimental fragmentation reanimates this essential historical figure.

Distinct from the shekhinah, Bruriah is extant in *volcano* as an historical figure, not a conceptualization. As the single female voice quoted in the Talmud, she entered the exclusively male territory of midrash, thereby striving for equality in interpreting Judaic holy texts. When her husband allegedly solicited the aid of a male student to seduce her, Bruriah's voice was silenced and she was branded as an immoral harlot. In *volcano*, she acts as amanuensis and vessel of gnosis for the contemporary daughter/wife/mother speaker.

In "Turn and Return," Part VII of *volcano* where readers discover the details of Bruriah's life amid Ostriker's address of the erasure of female Biblical scholars, the daughter/wife/mother tells of her own isolation, of a self fragmented in relation to others, even among the crowd. "I am alone at the party / the gaiety / of the falsely repentant." The Overlord Voice of God then responds, "*it is not your task / to judge but to speak / you are my teeth my tongue . . . I will be back— / I will bring comfort*" ("addendum to jonah"). Comfort does not arrive, which designates a space for the female speaker to fill. True to her appropriately rebellious nature, she concentrates on the silenced voice of Bruriah, whose husband, Rabbi Meir, apparently claimed that "'women are light-minded.'" Having discovered that she has been seduced by her husband's ruse, Bruriah committed suicide by hanging, and now Ostriker's formal concerns revivify her chosen ancestor.

Stylistically, Ostriker's stanzas contain non sequiturs, run-on formulations, and ample wordplay, the effect of which might be to generate a disruptive form that corresponds to the emotive protest and righteous rage that Ostriker navigates throughout the book, similar to what Bruriah felt on returning to consciousness and reacting to her husband's ruse. From the first poem, "volcano," to the later poem "the volcano breathes," the experimental nature of the book's form abounds with abrupt leaps, fragmentary renditions of experiences, and a variety of repetitions, all of which reinforce the idea of the manifold self. The breaking of the self—"attempting to touch we destroy we break we are broken"—entails a concomitant breaking of form.

Possibly referring to Muriel Rukeyser's *The Gates* (1976), Ostriker's speaker continues to protest the rabbis' double-standard: "but as for me / their gates stand closed / fastened against me // what must I do outside here" (36). Without the standard mark signifying a question, the daughter/wife/mother asks how a woman can arrive at anything but conventional religious dogma if she is required to remain "outside here," firmly beyond the pale of scholarly interrogation and therefore not knowable—insofar as that may be possible—to herself or to her world. Bruriah's voice shadows these lines. To have been invited into the boys' club, as Bruriah was, only to be forced out by destructive trickery resulted in the erasure of Bruriah's voice from Talmud and from history.

The experimental forms abounding throughout *volcano* culminate in "the volcano breathes," which opens Part VIII, "the volcano and the covenant." Comprised of formal variation—from brackets that posit either definitional elements or alternative word choices to lineation liberated from the left-hand margin—this poem is a tour de force in postmodern poetics. With a (subjectless) verbal trajectory, the poem begins: "coughs" is followed by the silence of ample white space before the word is repeated, completed, "coughs up" (87). Who (or what) is coughing up is not clear, but that verb takes readers back to the second section of the book's initial poem, "volcano," when the speaker indicates that the volcano "coughs out // hot beauty / thick and magnificent rage" (4). The act that has been transpiring for more than eighty pages, voiding the self of anger, loneliness, society's inequalities/iniquities, now moves into a new dimension. Voiding opens a space by which the speaker may now enter into her subconscious mind, her interior self. This subconscious self is compared to a *geniza*, or storage place for sacred documents that discuss God, for one of the things that the daughter/wife/mother-of-tensile-strength speaker has been coughing up is the received version of the Overlord. Without voiding herself of this conditioned prototype, she cannot substantiate her alternative female God. "the mind can't / throw anything holy away," she says.

In run-on form and with an emphasis on "she," she then offers "let it stay let it be she   let it wait." Gender maintains centrality, especially since the speaker has been voiding the masculine-inflected Overlord from her consciousness.

The female source of power rises here in stature, and in radically deconstructed form in which wordplay receives ample attention:

repository [place of repose   in which to put/push/press/repress
                pinched   her moist red   disturbed
        rose there   her terebinth   grove misremembered but]

The subconscious "repository" leads to "place of repose," which, by this poem's end, the speaker seeks: "I do have a heavy burden / and cannot wait to put it down." "press" and "repress" are playfully interlaced, encouraging readers to consider how the book in its entirety has been a pressing against a nerve, and now, with the resultant coughing up, has led to a freedom from what is repressed, thus documenting a link relating to Bruriah, whose repression seems to have emanated from her entire culture, much as what the daughter/wife/mother speaker implies concerning her own desire to enter into scholarship and live on equal terms with her masculine counterparts. Those counterparts include "the naked [failures] fathers," a punning reference to Ostriker's *The Nakedness of the Fathers*. Thus the poem's abstractions and cognitive concerns are laid out before us in a feast of "papyrus crumbs" of things remembered and misremembered.

Yet ultimately this poem, the form of which is as much horizontal as vertical, posits a speaker who moves from abstract thought to visceral physicality. "oh god," pleads the daughter/wife/mother speaker, "yours and ours / it hurts." A page later, she repeats this, with variation:

        oh god, yours and ours, how they hurt so
        bring forth your uterine self? by yourself? is it time's nick?
            [time present]
    she so buried so erased so unlawful so forgot so swallowed

The cause of this pain is the aforementioned "heavy burden" of human nature, a burden that, despite loneliness and uncertainty, knowledge of death and ability to register, within the cinematic scope of potentialities formulated throughout *volcano*, how humanity has mismanaged just about everything that it has laid its greedy hands on, God declares is *"forbidden"* *"to put it down"* (89). *"the volcano breathes"* clarifies that bewilderment that becomes the wonder of not-knowing, of remaining within uncertainty in which the imagination is free to roam and play—even if the general subject matter is of dire consequence and even if the Overlord, as demonstrated by the poem's final line, *"to put it* [the 'heavy burden'] *down is forbidden,"* once again has the last word.

The Overlord is ultimately only confronted, not replaced. Ostriker's positing of a female alternative remains shadow play. Though she indicates in some of the most viscerally affecting lines of the book that "when she [the female alternative to Overlord] comes it will not be from heaven, it will be up from the cunts and breasts / it will be from our insane sad fecund obscure mothers / it will be from our fat scrawny pious wild ancestresses . . . ," the masculine Overlord maintains power. "What reaches?" the wife/ mother speaker asks in "aperture." "What answers? From time to time something does answer. Like the surface tension in a cup of silence, trembling. What do I imagine is happening?" What God is and what we are, what we are doing, and how we arrived here are, of course, unanswerable. Yet the genius of Ostriker's *the volcano sequence* is that, even knowing the odds are against her, she asks the questions, confronts all manner of conglomerate power sources, has the courage to persist despite knowing that her project may end in failure. "interlude: bus driver" measures the impossibility of Ostriker's task. "do you know why the Lord made this world? [the driver] asks / I shake my head and look anticipatory / for his own *Glory!* she says. For his *glory!"* Glory of "three beggars wrapped in plastic." Glory of "boys of fourteen . . . [who] pass through villages [in Central Africa] scything the fingers and hands from women and sometimes older men." Glory of "tens of thousands / of refugees cross[ing] the border / like vapor from morning to dusk." Glory of hung Bruriah, of "Dido [who] immolates herself for love / Lucrece [who] stabs herself for shame." And glory of "the child . . . born / wet // and spills over into grandchild" who "will learn / to say hello to say ball / to say go up," just the way the daughter/wife/ mother-of-tensile-strength will, passing through a world of unfathomable pain and riches, a world depicted in states of fragmented incomprehensibility punctuated by momentary visions of satisfactory completion.

Ostriker was among the scholars and poets who gathered in an April 2008 conference to answer a vital (and absurd) question: "Why Study Women's Poetry?" Her talk, "Why Study Women's Poetry—Are You Kidding?" concerned women poets' attempt to transform the paradigms of Western civilization by moving through boundaries of form and style, meandering via non-narrative and fragmentary forms hospitable to poems of radical spirituality. Nothing short of locating the sacred in the physical world and rewriting history would do. I, along with the crowd gathered at St. Francis College in Brooklyn on a Saturday morning, were visibly affected both by Ostriker's ideas and her playful and humorous presentation, her pizzazz. In the Q&A after, I asked, "I'm wondering how you might define genius in our time?" Ostriker remarked on H.D.'s ear for music, Dickinson's intrepid imagination, Blake's political engagement, Shakespeare's fluid soul. She mentioned Ginsberg and Rukeyser, and I thought how each of the poets she listed had once been considered uniquely qualified to expose readers to what were, in their times, radically experimental forms. I wondered how Ostriker related these writers' bold forms to the personal voice that is found in each of their works. As it turns out, Ostriker had already written about that in *American Poetry Review*.

In her 2001 essay "Beyond Confession: The Poetics of Postmodern Witness," Ostriker reviewed three contemporary books by women poets, in the process demonstrating her admiration for experimental forms, rejecting "master narratives," and providing a possible reason for why she rejects—consciously, at least— postmodern literary theory, such as that of Roland Barthes. "Postmodern witness as I see it is a marriage of opposites," she writes:

> It employs the fragmented structures and polyglot associations originating in Eliot's *Waste Land*, Pound's *Cantos,* and Williams's *Paterson*, those epitomes of high modernism. Like them too, it reaches toward the objectively encyclopedic. Like them, it rejects master narratives. It refuses to pretend to coherence. But where high modernism rejects the autobiographical "I," [Adrienne Rich, Carolyn Forché, and Sharon Doubiago] retain it. . . . In the poetry I am looking at here, it is crucial that the poet is *present* and *located* in the poem. The poet is not simply a phantom manipulator of words but a confused actual person, caught in a world of catastrophe that the poem must somehow both mirror and transcend. (35)

Clearly Ostriker does not reject outright "fragmented structures" or "polyglot associations," but she does distrust expedient "coherence," a distrust found and exemplified by many postmodern contemporary poets. What Ostriker contests, then, is not incoherence, per se, but the disparagement and demotion of the "autobiographical 'I,'" that essential sign of postwar American confessional poetics. She traces the deflation of the "I" back to "Eliot's 'extinction of personality,' Pound's 'persona,'" which she maintains are "evasive" (35). It appears that Ostriker is in agreement with much that postmodernism has to offer—so long as the sanctity of the "I" is retained. Therefore it is not Barthes's emphasis on the value of fragmentation that Ostriker might object to; rather, it is his idea concerning the death of the author that is at issue. Thus, what I see as relevant to Ostriker's poetics, particularly that found in *the volcano sequence*, is a union of a poetics of fragmented incoherence and American first person poetry, a contextualizing of elements of postmodern poetics within the alignment of the confessional, personal "I."

People who exhibit qualities of genius are adept at amalgamation, which is what I see Ostriker doing in *the volcano sequence*, where she presents first-person speakers who generate positive obscurity reflected in the poems' experimental forms. This imbrication of the personal "I" and experimentation aligns her with Emerson's category of "[Wo]Man Thinking," "the active soul," which, in recognizing and speaking of truth, "is genius" (Emerson 59). Since the Latin *genius* translates into "procreative divinity" from *genare*, "to beget," poets of genius might be said to birth divinity—the raising of reader consciousness via contact with a rich and particular use of poetic language—in our midst. Such a birthing is not abstract principle in *the volcano sequence*; it is the book's primary intention. "we will have to struggle so hard / to birth you," the wife / mother's words from "earth: the shekhinah as amnesiac," is no whimsical foray into some airy fairyland. "it will be up from the cunts and breasts" is indicative of the physical act that will result in transfiguration, an act that may take place only within the female body / female consciousness.

Undeniably a feminist poet, Ostriker also embraces postmodern techniques, as evinced in *the volcano sequence*. To not acknowledge her experimental, postmodernist qualities is to refuse to see her genius in its full radiance. With its political commitment, fluidity of form, and imaginative shapeliness, Ostriker's work is aptly witnessed as *apotropaion*, as a configuration of Blake's "Poetic Genius" as "every where call'd the Spirit of Prophecy" (1). Embedded in the humility, love, and compassion for her fellows, wild patience, reverence for the natural world, and honor of the dead, prophecy radiates forth in a multitude of voices that, for nearly five decades, have expressed disdain for war and double-standard politics, have supported gender, racial, and sexual equality, and have laid claims that reach their apotheosis of expression via the fragmentary qualities found in *the volcano sequence*. With the fragment, linearity is put aside, an action that compromises the stranglehold of rhetorical argumentation, placing in its stead language as liberated enterprise, sonic aura. What Ostriker has accomplished in *the volcano sequence* is nothing less than seamlessly integrating the personal "I," and all its attendant sociopolitical resonance, with experimental forms of the highest order.

Works Cited

Adams, Susan Rushing. "An Interview with Alicia Ostriker." *Sojourn: A Journal of the Arts* 18 (2005).

Barthes, Roland. "The Death of the Author." In *Image—Music—Text*, 142–48. Translated by Stephen Heath. New York: Hill and Wang, 1977.

Barthes, Roland. *The Neutral.* New York: Columbia University Press, 2005.

Barthes, Roland. *Roland Barthes by Roland Barthes.* Translated by Richard Howard. Berkeley: University of California Press, 1994.

Blake, William. *The Complete Poetry & Prose of William Blake*, edited by David V. Erdman. New York: Doubleday, 1988.

Emerson, Ralph Waldo. "The American Scholar." In *Emerson's Prose and Poetry: A Norton Critical Edition*, edited by Joel Porte and Saundra Morris, 56–69. New York: W. W. Norton, 2001.

The Holy Bible: Authorized King James Version. Iowa Falls: World Publishing, 1989.

Oktenberg, Adrian. "Incandescent Clarity." *Women's Review of Books* 19, nos. 10/11 (July 2002): 35–36.

Ostriker, Alicia. "Beyond Confession: The Poetics of Postmodern Witness." *American Poetry Review* 30, no. 2 (March/April 2001): 35–39.

Ostriker, Alicia. *The Crack in Everything.* Pittsburgh: University of Pittsburgh Press, 1996.

Ostriker, Alicia. *The Mother/Child Papers.* Boston: Beacon Press, 1986.

Ostriker, Alicia. *For the Love of God: The Bible as an Open Book.* New Brunswick, NJ: Rutgers University Press, 2007.

Ostriker, Alicia. *The Nakedness of the Fathers: Biblical Visions and Revisions.* New Brunswick, NJ: Rutgers University Press, 1994.

Ostriker, Alicia. *The Old Woman, the Tulip, and the Dog.* Pittsburgh: University of Pittsburgh Press, 2014.

Ostriker, Alicia. *Stealing the Language: The Emergence of Women's Poetry in America*. Boston: Beacon Press, 1986.

Ostriker, Alicia. *the volcano sequence*. Pittsburgh: University of Pittsburgh Press, 2002.

Plato. *The Symposium*. Translated by Walter Hamilton. New York: Viking Penguin, 1951, 58–65.

Seaman, Donna. "The Poetics of Womanhood." *Booklist* (March 1, 2002): 1,086.

Shakespeare, William. *Hamlet*. Edited by G. R. Hibbard. Oxford World Classics. Oxford, UK: Oxford University Press, 2008, 218.

Stevens, Wallace. *The Palm at the End of the Mind: Selected Poems and a Play*. Edited by Holly Stevens. New York: Vintage, 1972.

Whitman, Walt. "Song of Myself." *Leaves of Grass*. Norton Critical Edition. Edited by Sculley Bradley and Harold W. Blodgett, 88. New York: W. W. Norton, 1973.

CYNTHIA HOGUE

On Ethical Poetics
The Example of Alicia Ostriker

> In the dream, Alicia Ostriker stands on a small rise in a luminous
> light, which surrounds her like an aura, and pronounces, "There will
> be peace in the Middle East." Then the dreamer wakes. There had
> been some new violence in the Middle East. Perhaps, the dreamer
> thinks, her dream might be prescient. Who better to stand as a
> prophetic figure in a dream of peace than Alicia Ostriker? The
> dreamer writes to her of this dream, and it so happens that Ostriker
> answers from Tel Aviv, where she is touring with a group of
> prominent Jewish intellectuals and activists organized by J Street.
> They are meeting both Israeli and Palestinian leaders to discuss
> possibilities for peace.
> AUTHOR'S NOTE

Alicia Ostriker opens her signature collection of essays on poetry,
Dancing at the Devil's Party: Essays on Poetry, Politics, and the Erotic,
with a bold defense of the cultural importance of the art:

> "Poetry makes nothing happen," said W. H. Auden, but there are
> those of us who disagree. Poetry can tear at the heart with its
> claws, make the neural nets shiver, flood us with hope, despair,
> longing, ecstasy, love, anger, terror. It can help us think more lu-
> cidly. It can force us to laugh. Poetry can, as Conrad puts it, make
> us *see*. It can also, like Rilke's torso of Apollo, tell us that we must
> change our lives. From time to time, some of us believe, poetry
> changes the world. I am of this (perhaps dotty) persuasion and I
> have always enjoyed the work of visionary artists dissatisfied with
> the rule of "things as they are[.]"[1]

Among the defining concerns of Ostriker's own work, from her
development as a major Second Wave feminist poet and critic to her
later feminist reconsiderations of Judaism, has been the earnest be-
lief that poetry—and art more generally—can help change the

thinking that structures enculturated patterns of dominance and violence. The wry, parenthetical self-deprecation in the passage above signals an awareness of her idealism's broad brush, but it doesn't qualify or diminish it. Poetry helps us to think more clearly. It helps our brains to re-pattern, our "neural nets" to shiver awake. It helps us *see* and feel things we'd otherwise miss. These are all heartfelt assertions, but they are also, I suggest, a considered *choice* to embrace a set of beliefs that offers ways of approaching the world that are fundamentally constructive and creative, rather than unconstructive and destructive.

In a prescient essay on the poet as postmodern witness, published on the eve of 9/11 in 2001, Ostriker writes of the challenges of remaining life-affirming despite the devastations of our times:

> To the famous declaration of Theodore Adorno that there can be no poetry after Auschwitz, a possible response is that there *must* be poetry after Auschwitz. Not to go on with poetry would be like not going on with life: a surrender to the powers of human destruction.[2]

Although her own poetry encompasses historically based grief and despair, she has passionately refused to let them dominate the tenor of her work. Writing poetry equates, in the passage above, with "going on with life." She wouldn't *dream* of "surrender." It is not wrong to subordinate art to history's horrors, she reasons, alluding to the influential teachings of Talmudic ethics, but she urges us not to stop there, for "the struggle [for peace and justice] can neither be won nor abandoned."[3]

That point is a crucial concern to which she returns the following year in the book-length, visionary *the volcano sequence* (2002). In "the volcano breathes," a poem that touches on "labor" as a dual trope—for birthing a child, and for the longing to lay one's burdens down that the knowledge of suffering engenders—the speaker admits the following:

> words of the mouth meditations of the heart
> from the source the desire
> is to flow without cease
>
> I do have a heavy burden
> and cannot wait to put it down

The passage can be read both as a statement of a poetics and an ethos, a way of being. Isn't it the hope of any wordsmith to set down words that flow directly from, as Ostriker has it here, "the heart"? But all that desire to be a conduit "from the source," however sincere, is an aesthetic, even moral pressure on the poet, who—wearily, humanly—"cannot wait to put it down" at last. She is told in no uncertain terms, however, in a variation of the Talmudic thinking referenced above, that "*to put it down is forbidden.*"

This exchange in brief, structured like a conversation between self and God, is a dynamic that lies at the core of Ostriker's oeuvre. She explores the possibilities for poetic engagement—the impact of words in the world—in formally complex, sometimes hybrid poems that interweave Biblical midrash (commentary), postmodern collage, fragmented narrative, apostrophe, and an at-times anguished speaker's ongoing protest of "things as they are." Ostriker's art tracks one poet's struggle, the witnessing, the transmuting, the act of contemplative analysis that her poetry often entails: these are places where her poetics and ethics *fuse.* It is this confluence of concerns as they meet in her poetry, what I am calling her *ethical* poetics, that I want to consider more closely in this brief essay.

In the Combat Zone

Ostriker's assertion that "poetry can help us think more lucidly" is literally illuminated in a powerful poem about the profession of helping people think clearly, that is, teaching. As a teaching poet myself, reading—and teaching—"The Class" over the twenty years since it was published in *The Crack in Everything* (1996), I'm still moved to tears by its riveting study of what is, in fact, the ethical pedagogy that today's creative writing teaching profession in public universities often requires. For twenty years, often to my mortification, I have been unable to wrap up a poetry writing class without tearing up, and *this* poem explains *why* to me. Into the overarching narrative of the teacher's compassion for her students, Ostriker makes collages of quotes of their words, so we hear them and glimpse their bravado, humor, and resilience. We also glimpse what they're up against. The poem begins with the teacher's embedded reportage from the "combat zone," punctuated by the students' differing perspectives so that, like a prism fracturing light into a full spectrum, the text reflects multiple voices and views. The potential dominance of the teacher's version of her students is thus refracted, interrupted, and reframed by her students themselves. This reframing upturns the normative classroom hierarchy of teacher-student. The field of the poem enlarges to embrace both comic and tragic registers, for example the broad comedic banter of New Jersey students qualified by the stark pathos of their circumstances. Tony Hoagland has recently characterized this striking element in Ostriker's oeuvre as her unique "ability to unite rawness and erudition."[4]

"The Class" opens with understatement, but in fact, like the epic genre to which it is surely heir, also in media res. I'll quote the opening at some length to give a sense of the juxtaposition of the teacher's contextualizing comments and the students' quoted quips (in italics):

We say things in this class. Like why it hurts.
But what they say outside of class is different; worse.
The teacher hears tales from the combat zone
Where the children live, conscripted at birth,
In dynamited houses. Like all draftees,
They have one job, survival,
And permit themselves some jokes.
Like my father hits the bottle . . .
And my mother. In my office a sofa,
Books, prints, disorder on the desk.
Everything paid for, chosen, they know that. . . .
Their nervous eyes glide over printed poems
I hand them, but nothing exactly sticks—
The black student pulled apart by his loyalties
Whose bravado breaks like a shoelace. . . .
The homosexual drummer tapping out
A knee tune, wagging his Groucho brows.
Hey, you ought to meet my mom real soon.
'Cause when I tell her, she's gonna die.

The teacher listens to the students' "common stories"—the choice of the word *common* both precisely descriptive and dramatically ironic—of surviving incest, rape, abuse of all sorts, attempted suicide. She knows that, in challenging her students to *Write what makes you afraid to write,*" she "helps them descend to hell." Condensed into a word functioning equally at colloquial and mythic levels, "hell" is what the students have to write about: "They'll write about that, or nothing."

As portrayed in "The Class," the poetic process and praxis—confronting and expressing one's *material*—entails, as Ostriker implies, embarking on a hero's journey. In the structure of that narrative, the teacher functions as ally and guide to her hero-students. She declares that her "job," as she underscores,

> . . . . is to give them permission
> To gather pain into language, to insist
> The critics are wrong, the other professors are wrong
> Who describe an art divisible from dirt,
> From rotten life. . . .

Suddenly, the prismatic frame of reference has shifted from sociocultural portrait of class-based teaching today to the spiritual terrors of the sacred and profane—of Pilgrim's progress, Saint's path to enlightenment, or the Soul before poetry's "house of judgment"—in the space of a line break. Rather than surrender to despair over art's powerlessness in "hell," which can render great pain insurmountable, Ostriker asserts the connection of art to all with which "dirt" is metonymically associated. The students may be negotiating violence, rejection, and abuse, but as the teacher believes, when they bear witness to that "rotten life"—rather than repress it, formalize experience into the ritual-like language of poetic patterning—they empower themselves to break the taboos that have kept them silent. They themselves, like the hero emerging from the underworld with the necessary knowledge to succeed, might be in a position to help others. "*Write for the sake of the silenced*," the teacher tells them.

We might presume that the idealism of the "The Class," like truth in the poem, is "*mighty above all things*," but the poem shifts once more, concluding on a note that not only reframes the teacher's narrative vision, but grounds it in the soil of the students' lived experience, from which, in fact, they cannot escape. The teacher at once believes "Against evidence" that "Poetry heals, or redeems suffering," and acknowledges but a line later that "Perhaps it is not the poet who is healed." Perhaps it will be a reader someday who is healed, while the poets themselves, these heroic, traumatized survivors, may never be fully healed, whether they write poems or not.

The daunting truth is that it's all the students have to write, the specificity of their particular *hells*, and nothing more. That is a brutal reality so subtly slipped in that I hardly noticed it all these years. The teacher—who has encouraged her students in every way to speak their truths—stops herself from saying to them, "*Great is truth and mighty above all things.*" The poem does not end with such soaring rhetoric, its penultimate line, but with the acknowledgment that the teacher "would never say so in a class." Why ever not? And why admit it in the last line? Ostriker doesn't say so in the poem, but we can read between the lines. Perhaps the teacher refrains from waxing biblical, because such a rhetorical flourish wouldn't ring true to her students. Or, perhaps she recognizes that her belief that poetry heals is *not* backed by empirical evidence, and as an act of pure faith, it might ring hollow. Although she has in *good* faith assumed her role with the students, the teacher in the poem embraces—and Ostriker enacts—an honesty with self that has shifted her position by the end of the poem. Its idealistic brilliance has dimmed enough that we can see it cast in relief. In the poem's final line, the teacher's dominance is implicitly in check as she meets her students where they began: she is silent.

Ostriker's portrait of ethical pedagogy is as poignant as it is sharp. The teacher arrives in a place of humility, where she acknowledges both the possibilities and limitations of any class, reasonably what she can and cannot do with and for her students. Part of the mighty truth of this remarkable poem can be located in Ostriker's acute account of how the teacher's beliefs come to be tempered by truth. I know of no other treatment of the artist as teacher that equals "The Class" in analytical breadth or thematic complexity.

In Purgatory

The narrative pivots that Ostriker enacts to bring "The Class" to such profound moral insight characterize her ethical poetics more generally. To consider that notion, I want to explore as exemplary one of the poems of "interlude" that punctuate the larger project of spiritual inquiry in *the volcano sequence*, "interlude: the avenue of the americas." The poem opens with a dazzling conceit of the city as devouring mouth—the cabs are flitting "tongues" and the skyscrapers grinning "teeth." This trope morphs quickly into a sustained riff sketching the problematic consumption of dwindling natural resources in the name of "need." The poem ranges in its sketches of such "need," pointedly raising questions about how our very use of the word is contextualized by social position and class. The loggers clear-cutting Oregon's virgin forests "need jobs," but is their need the same kind or degree as the East Coast "intellectuals" who "need the special sections / of the New York Times"? As the poem sardonically underscores, "everybody needs what they can get / and more."

Ostriker stops short of cynicism with a turn to personal lyric. A speaker is introduced, clearly an author-surrogate, out on an ordinary evening in New York with friends for dinner. The women encounter a figure of consequential "need," in fact, an actual and horrifying *neediness*, which begins to flesh out further connotations of the word:

> ... Yesterday walking
> between fifty-third and fifty-second
>
> on the avenue of the americas at twilight on my way
> to a good restaurant with good friends I passed
> three beggars wrapped in plastic. Why not say
>
> beggars?
> Why invent novelty phrases like "the homeless"
> as if our situation were modern and special
>
> instead of ancient and normal,
> the problem of greed and selfishness?

The passage is grounded in reality-based details of where the speaker is walking (midtown Manhattan), when (yesterday evening at twilight), with whom (good friends) and to where (a good restaurant), but Ostriker has deftly infused the anecdotal with the mythic. The poem moves into a meditation on the problem of having a language adequate to the spiritual encounter of an "I" with an absolutely abject "Thou." The speaker may be culturally privileged, but she is also symbolically *placed* on the Avenue of the Americas, and thus in some sense, she is out of place—quite literally *ec-static*. Is this a vision? Have we stepped out into Whitman's democratic crowds or Emma Lazarus's "huddled masses"? Or, given the poem's adoption of unrhymed tercets, have we entered a postmodern, Dantesque *purgatorio*? The speaker is forced to confront her own privilege, reflected back to her large and distorted, as in a funhouse mirror, in the rheumy eyes of the beggar. The poem repeats the word "beggar," gives it its own line, transforming linguistic contemplation of the word's historical use into a rhetorical—which is to say an unanswerable—question. The repeated word beggars the imagination with its intensified, plosive power.

We readers must pause, just as the speaker in the poem has. Then, also like the speaker in the poem, we must look:

> I put money in the woman's cup
> though I didn't like her facial sores
> her drowned eyes bobbed to the surface
>
> as if they believed for a second
> something new was about to happen
> but nothing was
>
> so the eyes sank rapidly back
> like crabs into sand, and sorrow
> pressed into me like a hot iron

The speaker sees the beggar in all her decrepitude, reminding us, but more graphically and without humorous intervention, of the "dirt" and "rotten life" from which the teacher in "The Class" believed art cannot be divided. In "interlude: the avenue of the americas," that inclusion creates the tension that charges the poem. Although the speaker doesn't "like" what she sees, she doesn't, for a long moment, look or walk away. The beggar, however, does not return her gaze, not because she can't, but because she has sized the speaker up and found her *wanting*. She takes the money but refuses the offer of a compassionate face-to-face encounter. The beggar's refusal handily strips the speaker of any possible illusion that the charitable gift she is making will change anything in the beggar's life or alter the structure of their encounter.

What begins in anecdote, develops as a portrait of a humane encounter, and veers sharply into something more ethically complex and disturbing. The poem acknowledges that the beggar is dehumanized by her condition, spelling it out (her eyes "like crabs into sand"). But as well, the speaker herself seems, at least implicitly, reduced when her charitable gesture—she alone steps up to give money—is rebuffed. She is described as being branded, as if tortured or marked by her ensuing sorrow, at which point, she breaks her gaze, hurries away to catch up with her friends, who are off "chatting so as not to be embarrassed / by the sight of charity // the rotting odor of need." But does she return to her life the same?

The scrutiny Ostriker brings to bear on this scene is piercing, scalpel-like in its analytical precision, rigorous in its moral insight. Each position is examined and exposed. No illusion survives Ostriker's searing inquiry.

Among the uncomfortable questions the poem raises is whether, since the speaker brought "nothing" new to the beggar, it was any better to have looked and felt the pain than to have walked away immediately, like her friends? What difference did caring make, or for that matter, the friends' implacable indifference? Haven't the two positions produced the same results for the beggar: nothing has changed? But perhaps we cannot say the same of the speaker herself, who has been chastened, psychically marked by the realization that she brought "nothing" to the beggar that the woman hadn't seen many times before, that her gift of money cannot touch the root causes of abject poverty.

Thus, what also changes in the course of the poem is our sense of the meaning of the word, the discriminating differences in kind that Ostriker draws between the "need" with which the poem opens and "the rotting odor of need" with which it closes. The speaker's position, moreover, the stability of her privileged vantage point, the solidity of her complacence, has been unsettled. Her impulsive act of charity calls into question the normative hierarchy of donor and beggar: like teacher and students in "The Class," in "interlude" speaker and beggar end on a par. Ostriker deconstructs the oppressive model of class difference, that of dominance and submission, for the donor refrains from dominating and the beggar refuses to submit to her patron by displaying gratitude. In "interlude," moreover, Ostriker refrains from indicating what she has elsewhere theorized as a "healing alternative" to oppression, which art can help us to imagine. She writes of ritual poetry in spiritual circles, for example,

> For poet and reader-participant alike, ritual poetry implies the possibility of healing alternatives to dominance-submission scenarios. It suggests nonoppressive models of the conjunction between religion and politics, usually by reimaging the sacred as immanent rather than transcendent. (*Dancing* 17)

Something of this dynamic is at work in "interlude"—especially, it seems to me, the speaker's encounter with the immanence of sacred poverty—but the poem resists positing a clear resolution. Its insight is bleaker, its honesty unflinching: parity of structure and place can be represented, poetically wrought, but social parity, imagining alternatives to oppressive social structures, is more elusive. Ostriker acknowledges that in the encounter explored in "interlude," no healing has happened, but the speaker is alert to something to which she had previously been blind. It's a start.

At the end of the poem, the speaker is looking up at the "primrose and lilac" sky at sunset, seeing the "cloud bouquets" that the skyscrapers are mirroring far above her, like her former place in a world mirroring its pastoral and now-distant beauty back to her. She, however, is down on the gritty, urban ground with the beggar, where the smell fills her nostrils as she takes her leave. The poem does not release her from the effects of her encounter, and it doesn't release us readers into lyrical beauty or compassionate insight. It won't let us forget what we have seen. Like the speaker's, our psyches are marked.

No Heaven[5]

These poems are exemplary of Ostriker's ethical poetics. They refuse resolutions that might comfort us with too-facile reason. On the contrary, they do the difficult job of discomfiting us, and though we might dream, they remind us that the struggle to address want and create real parity and peace can neither be won nor abandoned.

Notes

Portions of this essay, in an earlier version, were included in my essay "Another Postmodernism: Toward an Ethical Poetics," *How2* 1, no. 7 (Spring 2002). Electronic journal archived at http://www.how2journal.com/archive/

1. Alicia Ostriker, *Dancing at the Devil's Party: Essays on Poetry, Politics, and the Erotic* (Ann Arbor: University of Michigan Press, 2000), i. Hereafter cited parenthetically in text as *Dancing*, followed by the page number.

2. Alicia Ostriker, "Beyond Confession: The Poetics of Postmodern Witness," *APR* 30, no. 2 (March/April 2001): 35 [35–39].

3. Ibid., 35. As Ostriker clarifies, this ethos, to which she'll return in her poetry, is drawn from the Talmudic *Ethics of the Fathers*: "It is not incumbent on you to finish the task. Neither are you free to give it up."

4. Tony Hoagland, "'I Would Like To Repent But I Cannot': The Poems of Alicia Ostriker," *Poet Lore* 11, nos. 1/ 2 (Spring/Summer, 2016): 108. A version of this essay is included in this volume.

5. *No Heaven*, published in the first years of the Iraq War, takes its title and epigraph from the John Lennon song "Imagine," the first line of which is "Imagine there's no heaven."

DAISY FRIED

Measureless Pleasure, Measureless Pain
Alicia Ostriker's Men

Alicia Ostriker: poet, critic, scholar, teacher, and informing all these, feminist. Striking, then, how often men show up in her poems, and not just men as stick figures, place-holders, clutches for shifts in tone and pacing. Ostriker's men are generally complex characters who talk back. They fall into several categories: (1) family members (mostly husband and son, but especially husband), (2) men in the news or in history (Nixon, soldiers, William Lloyd Garrison), (3) other men in passing—cab drivers, students, workers—and, (4) giving the husband a run for his money, artists.

Here's a poem from *No Heaven*:

CROSSTOWN

Back in New York I grab a taxi at Port Authority,
A young Jamaican guy, then a big Af-Am guy in
A monster silver SUV tries to cut him off but he dashes
Round in front like a fox and then can't move
So we're sitting in the traffic people leaning
On their horns all around us and the big guy comes
Out and starts threatening my driver—*I'm just out
Of jail.—So go back to jail.* No love lost it happens
All the time, *They think they are tough and we are
Nothing, we think they are worse than nothing.*
He's been driving two years saving to go to school
To catch up on his computer design skills, the wife
Got impatient and cheated on him, he still sees his
Little daughter who is so pretty and smart she can
Read at the age of four. He'd like to be a better
Christian but working this job he gets in situations
Where he uses bad language. Next day another
Cabbie this one older we talk about Iraq and about power
I say we are seeing the defects of democracy
He says he doesn't believe in democracy democracy
Is for the rich.

Went to Sheila's, we walked on Riverside Drive as
The sun was setting bathing the high limbs of the elms
Coral, the trunks sinking into darkness, we were
Happy together and other walkers also looked happy
Trees tranquilly surviving blight seemed fine
A man passed us with a poodle so elegant it looked
Like a model on a runway.

Small kid on the crosstown bus, a high clear voice:
If you kick somebody, people won't be your friend.
Woman next to me carries a large flat manila envelope
Her makeup is violent her middle-aged hair is lacquered
Her coat olive green embroidered cashmere expensive
I think art? photography? then I see the envelope says
X-rays, so it's cancer.

The poet rushes around New York, a twenty-first-century Frank
O'Hara in cabs and a bus, instead of on foot in shoe leather. We get
a lot of information about America in the pair of cabbie stories.
There's the dangerous-to-touch story of the relations between
African-Americans and Jamaican immigrants. There's the Jamaican
guy's life in a snapshot. And there's the older cab driver, who is a sort
of oracle. These men are working class, human and likeable; they say
interesting things. The guy with the poodle? A nifty little walk-on
in the midst of a sort of pastoral-in-the-city respite with a friend.
Till we get to the kid on the bus, the poem is a vivacious montage,
both serious and light, with deft accelerations and downshifts in
velocity and feeling. The kid makes the poem completely change
direction. He's not where the poem is going, but he's the hinge that
lets the thing move. What he says is fun: we shouldn't kick anyone,
not because it's wrong but because of the repercussions: nobody
will like us if we kick them. Out of the mouths of babes: suddenly
this poem about difficulty and race and democracy in America is
also a poem about war, and specifically, in the context of this book
and this poem, about the current war. I love that this poem makes
this move, and I love that it doesn't stop there.

The final character to walk onstage—on-bus—is a woman, and
she is middle class, and the poet doesn't like her. She is looked at
differently than the men. She is physically described. By contrast,
the men are simply "young" or "big" or "older"—however, we can
picture them quite clearly because their surroundings, actions, or
props act as mirrors. Even the poodle is a kind of mirror for the

cameo dog walker. But: "Her makeup is violent her middle-aged hair is lacquered." The most sisterly of poets is being, well, unsisterly. It's a brilliant move. What's happening here is a recognition. We understand that the poet knows something about cancer because she immediately knows the secret of this woman's life once she sees the word "X-ray." And because this woman comes after the montage about class and race and the war, she also becomes a kind of emblem of America itself, its privileged and impervious surface, with a cancer inside. That the poet sees herself in the woman suggests that she sees herself, and by extension, the reader, as complicit in America's crimes. The central figure in the poem, then, is the woman on the bus. But she could not do everything she has to do for this poem without all of the men setting her up. The men reflect her world; she exists in a world of men.

Ostriker's poem "Matisse, Too" appeared in *Poetry* in December 2006.[1]

MATISSE, TOO

Matisse, too, when the fingers ceased to work,
Worked larger and bolder, his primary colors celebrating
The weddings of innocence and glory, innocence and glory

Monet when the cataracts blanketed his eyes
Painted swirls of rage, and when his sight recovered
Painted water lilies, Picasso claimed

I do not seek, I find, and stuck to that story
About himself, and made that story stick.
Damn the fathers. We are talking about defiance.

This poem is about courage, about frailty, about how to keep going as an artist. And then—"Damn the fathers. We are talking about defiance." Damn the fathers. The phrase fascinates, and refuses to resolve into a simple idea. Is it a rejection of the patriarchy? Certainly that's one idea that's in the poem. And yet the father-artists have wedded innocence and glory, shown how to defy the loss of eyesight, how to control one's own narrative. They are inspiring and interesting. Could defying the patriarchy be this poet's big struggle, like Matisse's arthritis, Monet's cataracts, Picasso's story? Could it also mean—damn worrying about the patriarchy: it's not about gender, it's about art? Damn, then, these notions of how a contemporary woman artist is supposed to relate to the male masters? And even so, even still, damn the men? This poem contains all these ideas without resolving them.

Finally, *The Mother/Child Papers* is a sequence of poems and prose published in 1980 about the birth of a son in wartime—in this case it's 1970 and America has invaded Cambodia and shot its own children at Kent State. The men in this book-length poem are the son Gabriel, the husband, President Nixon, Dr. Keensmile, the condescending doctor who gives the poet Demerol without her permission during childbirth, boy students, boy soldiers, National Guardsmen, veterans. In the middle of it all, there is this extraordinary love poem:

> The door clicks. He returns to me.
> He brings fresh air in.
> We kiss, we touch. I am holding the flannel-wrapped baby.
> The girls run to him.
>
> He takes his jacket off and waltzes
> the weightless
> bundle over his shoulder.
> We eat dinner, and evening falls.
>
> I have bathed the girls. I walk by our broad bed.
> Upon it rests a man
> in a snow white shirt, like a great sleepy bird.
> Next to him rests his seed, his son.
>
> Lamplight falls on them both. If a woman looks, at such
> a sight, is the felt pang
> measureless pleasure?
> Is it measureless pain?

This poem is hard to talk about. It's so simple and at the same time mysterious. Pleasing domestic scene, happy family. That's the first two stanzas. The third stanza turns sexy, and eerie. A woman looks at her man, and he is animal and also Fatherhood with a capital F, and he is, in that white shirt, purity and civilization. He is intimately familiar and inaccessible. And then the fourth stanza—"*If* a woman looks . . ." She may not look. Anyone may recognize the feeling here, the shock of love that keeps getting renewed, the way that love is a hybrid thing made up of pleasure and of pain. It's a place of discomfort and excitement—just as a good poem is a place of discomfort and excitement. The man in this poem *is* the poem, because like a poem, he takes away the familiar, via the familiar. The poet lets him. She can't help letting him.

This is feminist poetry about living with men.

Note

1. Ostriker edited the poem when it appeared later in *The Book of Seventy* (Pittsburgh, 2009), where it became the middle of three poems grouped under the title "Ars Poetica." She removed the original title, and changed the last line to "Damn right. We are talking about defiance." I think these are equal versions with different things to say, as with the two versions of William Carlos Williams's "[The] Last Words of My [English] Grandmother" or the two versions of Yeats's "The Sorrow of Love" where it's hard to say one is better than the other; just that the poem's requirements had changed as (presumably) the poet changed.

JACQUELINE OSHEROW

Poetic Outrage/Poetic Grace
A Few Poems by Alicia Ostriker

It is rare to find outrage in genuinely valuable poetry. Outrage, after all, is not a subtle emotion, and poetry, for the most part, is a subtle medium. The problem of sacrificing neither intensity on the one hand nor the unique grace of the medium itself on the other is one that Alicia Ostriker manages to solve again and again in *The Book of Life: Selected Jewish Poems, 1979–2011*. She does this largely by turning the Bible on its head, often using its very poetry against itself. Take, for example, the poem "judgment," which I'll quote here in its entirety:

> One of these days
> oh one of these days
> will be a festival and a judgment
>
> and our enemies will be thrown
> into the pit while we rejoice
> and sing hymns
>
> Some people actually think this way

The only word for the stance of this poem is *chutzpadik*, since it effectively pits its own speaker's "judgment" against that not only of "some people," but of their imagined God. Divine "judgment" is rendered far less just than our speaker's "judgment." Thousands of years of mainstream religious belief and longing are implicitly marginalized by the speaker's stance of needing to insist that "some people *actually* (emphasis mine) think this way." The tradition and its God, in one fell swoop, become outliers in a landscape dominated by what is implicitly established as a far superior approach to "judgment." On the other hand, by calling God to judgment, Ostriker is actually placing herself directly in line with the patriarchs. After all, Abraham himself famously asks, "shall not the Judge of all the earth do right?" (Genesis 18:25 KJV). Ostriker pushes this tradition and its Yiddish-language, Eastern-European stepchild—a sarcasm-tinged irreverence—as far as it can go. She isn't hampered—as her ancestors probably would have been—by anxiety over some reactive, marauding *evil eye*. Ostriker is utterly fearless.

But Ostriker's difficulties with some of the Bible's "judgments" do not shut her off to its power. And though, in her anger, she declares in the poem, "psalm," "I will not play the harp / for your pleasure // I will not make a joyful / noise to you" and then "I pull my eyes away from the hills / I will not kill for you," in the next section of the poem she declares, very much in the spirit of the original psalmists, "You have made everything wondrous after its kind." The poem—like the psalms that inspired it—is an extremely ample one. Indeed, its ability to contain, simultaneously, both a sense of wonder and a sense of outrage endows it with the tension that gives it, finally, its depth. The outrage is far more potent when accompanied by a sense of awe; the conflicted relationship to God conveyed in a question like: "You have done enough, engineer / how dare we ask you for justice" is even more affecting in a stanza full of lavish description of natural beauty ("wren," "lions," "antelope," "butterfly"). The poem's power arises from this push and pull—this fury at God combined with supreme awe and gratitude.

After all, in our time, there are plenty of devout nonbelievers. Merely railing against the God of the Bible could, to some, seem simply quaint. But the combination of that outrage with true attraction—an attraction sometimes figured as physical (in another psalm, "I am waiting for you / in a bed of pleasure") becomes something else entirely. Once again, this is firmly rooted in Jewish tradition, which sees spiritual adhesiveness between God and Israel as the true message of the erotic language of the Song of Songs.

But at the same time, the insistent masculinity of that God is part and parcel of Ostriker's outrage. Toward the beginning of section I of "A Meditation in Seven Days" the speaker asks:

Why the chain of this nation matrilineal

When the Holy One, the One
Who created heaven and earth

Is utterly, violently masculine, with his chosen
Fathers and judges, his kings

and continues:

> —What were they all but men in the image
> Of God, where is their mother

The implication—that mothers humanize, while fathers incite and model violence—is both subversive and traditional. Ostriker embraces a traditional understanding of the feminine here; she seems to be saying that God's lack of a feminine partner in creation—that missing "mother"—is at the root of earthly violence.

When she goes on to focus on that mother figure—in section VI—the results are far more appealing.

> Our mothers' palms like branches lifted in prayer
> Lead our rejoicing voices, our small chorus
>
> Our clapping hands in the here and now
> In a world that is never over
>
> And never enough

Once mothers begin their "prayer," "rejoicing" enters the text. "The world" becomes not chaotic and destructive and prison-like, but "never enough." That it is both eternal and insufficient—"never over" and "never enough"—suggests the world's insatiable appetite for femininity.

In "What Is Needed after Food," the speaker figures herself as a mother. I suspect it is no coincidence that this is also the poem that contains the volume's most hopeful account of coexistence in the State of Israel, which we get through the coach of a victorious underdog soccer team:

> When someone asks how he feels about his team
> (A mix of Jews, Muslims, and one Nigerian,
>
> He himself is Druze), he punches the air
> And roars, *I beat them all! I beat Arafat! I beat Sharon!*
> *I show them we love each other!* We watch a while,
>
> The celebration is still going on when we quit
> To go back to the kitchen . . . .

But love is a good idea, we think, why on earth not.
Simple women that we are, simple mothers cleaning up
The kitchen after one meal to make it ready for the next.

Here, too, in the unending round of meals to be made, cleaned up, and made again, we are given a picture of a female contribution that is at once "never over" and "never enough." It's a lovely glorification of the domestic, but it, too, is complicated. After all, this volume contains many poems that object to the Jewish double standard of education for men and not for women. Section II of "A Meditation in Seven Days" is bitterly introduced by an epigraph from Rabbi Eleazar: "Whoever teaches his daughter Torah, / teaches her obscenity."

Once again, Ostriker turns a seemingly straightforward stance—her objection to women's exclusion from the roles of "Prophet, Judge, and King" and restriction to the domestic sphere—on its head. For one thing, her description of her friend and herself as "simple women" cannot be taken at face value. In the penultimate stanza of "What Is Needed after Food," she has told us,

My friend and I, we don't ask for much, we read Amichai,
We're not messianic, we don't expect utopia, which is anyway
Another name for a smiling prison.

Merely to track the quality of thought that leads from "utopia" to "smiling prison" is to recognize that the speaker is anything but "simple." "Read(ing) Amichai" or indeed any contemporary poet is hardly an activity associated with those who spend their lives in the kitchen. But Ostriker—poet that she is, intellectual that she is—claims the kitchen, owns the kitchen; she does not see the women's sphere and the intellectual sphere in opposition. I am reminded of a favorite character, Susan Garth in George Eliot's *Middlemarch*, who has her students "follow her about in the kitchen with their book and slate" (*Middlemarch*, kindle edition, 259). For Ostriker the kitchen is not incompatible with poetry and serious political, philosophical thought. What the kitchen does is humanize through caregiving and nurturing; what it does here, in this poem, is humanize the intellectual inheritance to which Ostriker is staking her own claim. She and her friend dismiss the "messianic," replacing thousands of years of Jewish longing, of passively awaiting a redeemer, with actively taking on the improvement of the world themselves, one nurturing meal at a time.

Ostriker's implication—that such care and nurturing humanize the world—extends to her readings of feminized symbols in Jewish lore from the city of Jerusalem (figured in Lamentations as a widow), to the mystical notion developed by Kabbalists of the feminine presence of God or Shekinah. She gives us a Jerusalem

> Who knits and frowns, going over and over her story.
> Sifting it, every detail memorized, magnified,
> Interpreted. How many lovers, what caresses, what golden
> Fornications, what children of brilliant intellect
> Sucking hard at her nipples.
> What warriors, what artists.

Once again, Ostriker subverts even as she maintains a certain traditional position. She attributes to Jerusalem qualities identified with the feminine ("going over and over her story"), as well as humorously alluding to those traditionally present in any Jewish-mother stereotype: that eagerness to discover, develop, and point out her children's "brilliant intellect." Ostriker also, however, brings in feminine qualities usually suppressed. That Jerusalem should focus on "golden / fornications" is once again highly subversive; merely putting the word "fornications" in Jerusalem's mind could certainly be construed as blasphemous. The word conveys illegitimacy, sexual activity unsanctioned by Jewish law. But if the word is calculated to shock, that shock is implicitly contrasted to a lack of shock on the part of the "violently masculine," of God Himself, who tolerates and indeed demands violence. Ostriker also gives us a Shekinah designed to shock: "when she comes it will not be from heaven, it will be up from the cunts and breasts." Here too, the shock we feel at a word like "cunts" is meant to force us to come to terms with what is truly outrageous, to question our shock at an old, earthy word in the face of our toleration of a "heaven" that "dances with hate."

Ostriker explicitly gives us more specific examples of our violent world in a number of outraged poems dated on Jewish holidays. In "during the bombing of Kosovo," dated "*Passover, 1999*," she tells us "above the hills bombs fall" and "roads crawl with tanks soldiers" and "refugees cross the border," ultimately asking "and you, you— / father of rain / what are you thinking." In "the fast," which is dated

"*Yom Kippur, 1999*," the first words are "we destroy we break we are broken."

But the final words of the final poem in the collection leave us with a much more positive and hopeful image of what is possible in the world:

> As if outside the synagogue we stood
> On holier ground in a perennial garden
> Jews like ourselves have just begun to plant.

That the "holier ground" is "outside the synagogue" is, of course, hardly surprising. But what is new is identifying "outside the synagogue" as a more desirable Jewish space, a "garden" for "Jews like ourselves." One might easily take "Jews like ourselves" to mean "women"—though I think Ostriker has deliberately left the phrase open to all those who would like to self-identify with the peaceful opposition. After reading poem after poem bemoaning the chaotic, violent state of the world, we are suddenly provided with a positive possibility. That this garden of "Jews like ourselves" is "perennial" inspires even more hope, suggestive of a desirable future of our own (and implicitly, not of God's) making, one that is in our control. Not only is it in our power "to plant" something that will last, something that will renew itself, something "perennial," we are told that planting has already—if only "just"—"begun."

TONY HOAGLAND

"I Would Like to Repent But I Cannot"
The Poems of Alicia Ostriker

Lately, I have been thinking about luck, and generations: the luck one artist or thinker has to be born at a particular juncture of historical circumstance in which people see her poetry and prose, find her writing relevant, and value her work. The misfortune of another artist, no less talented or serious, is to be ignored or peripheralized, viewed as absurd, heretical, or insignificant simply because he arrived too early or too late. What would have happened if Gertrude Stein or e. e. cummings had tried to publish their work forty years earlier, in 1870 rather than 1910? We must suspect that the world is full of geniuses never made visible because they were outside the range of contemporary taste. They simply never got an audition. This avenue of meditation, of course, also forces one to consider the politics of cultural destiny written into our skin color and gender.

In the United States, the late 1960s and '70s were the first decades when it might have been worth your while to try to be a woman poet, when, as Ostriker puts it, "some were deciding, although it had never before been possible to be both fully woman and fully poet, that they would turn, and stand, and fight" (*Stealing the Language* 58). Not that you were going to be *welcomed* by the 99-percent male literary world; nonetheless, the cultural tide had turned in so many ways that it was at least possible to publish your work; the politics of sex, the acceptance of the personal as political, and Second-Wave feminist thought were in such a state of wild fermentation, they would not be denied attention—and at last the audience for poetry by women was growing.

On the one hand, Alicia Ostriker's fate as a poet was to arrive at this particular moment of cultural blossoming, a moment when a

---

A version of this essay was published in *Poet Lore* 11, nos. 1/2 (Spring/Summer 2016).

breach had opened in the wall of male monopoly, and in the insular poetics of the '50s. As the child of idealistic New York immigrant socialists, she was well suited for the revolutionary temper of the times. She made her bones, so to speak, writing the poems of a politicized feminist humanism. She also adopted the stylistic idiom of the time, in which a rough colloquial texture and velocity verify the speaker's passion and sincerity. Here, for example, is the pithy, urgent beginning of "Insomnia": "But it's really fear you want to talk about / and cannot find the words / so you jeer at yourself // you call yourself a coward."

The way that many of Ostriker's poems seem to neatly fit the prosodic profile of the genre accounts for a certain degree of the invisibility she has suffered. Here are the antiwar poems, here the poems of mastectomy and sisterhood, the rendered accounts of gender prejudice; here is the narration of marginalized lives. And perhaps too, the rough, cadenced forcefulness of Ostriker's poems also rendered her work less visible than it would have been otherwise.

On the other hand, the timing *within* a generation is also relevant. If Ostriker had the fortune to be born into a cultural moment that made room (however reluctantly) for women's poetry, one could say that she also had the misfortune to come of age in the shadows of a full grove of eminent peers—Rich and Rukeyser, Plath and Sexton—whose presences filled the foreground of American readers' attention. Likewise, Ostriker had the bad luck to fall between the cracks generationally, between two waves of very strong women poets; first Rich, ('29) and Plath ('32), and then Olds ('42) and Glück ('43). The mind of the American reader has a limited capacity for the identities of artists. Such a cohort and such timing worked against the recognition of her singularity.

To be sure, Ostriker has carved a substantial career for herself. Two of her books have been finalists for the National Book Award. An active critic and a scholar of William Blake and the Bible, as well as a poet, she was a long-tenured professor at Rutgers University. On the other hand, Ostriker's work is not included in the major anthologies that easily come to mind: *The Oxford Anthology of American Poetry*, the latest edition of the *Norton* anthology, the Poulin Anthology, now edited by Michael Waters, the Friebert and Young *Longman Guide to Contemporary American Poetry*. To my knowledge, Ostriker's work is collected in none of them.

Timing and luck, luck and timing. Perhaps because it was camouflaged in the prosodic garb of '70s feminist poetry, the distinctness of her work was difficult to see. But, in fact, Ostriker's work IS distinctive—not so much in manners as in rhythm and temperament, most notably in the diversity and breadth of its passions. As well as advocating for political justice, she is a poet of Eros; as well as being sexual, she is unabashedly religious in temperament; all of these subject matters are modulated by the poet's canny adroitness with depth psychology and myth. Few poets parse experience in so many directions, and with such intense scrutiny.

Part of Ostriker's capaciousness springs from a brainy streak in her temperament, a trait somewhat camouflaged by the proletarian slant of her discourse. Genuinely philosophical concerns often surface in her poems: inquiries into the nature of knowing, the human (in)ability to apprehend reality, the spiritual imperative that underlies all living things—such themes insistently mingle with, and sometimes even supersede, the stuff of social conscience. In the poem "Marie at Tea," for example, the speaker says, "You remember the extremes / Wittgenstein says / There is no such thing as ordinary / Experience." Such moments fit perfectly well into the poems they belong to, but they bespeak an intellectual appetite for pure idea above and beyond the concerns of history, gender, or social justice.

"Still Life: A Glassful of Zinnias on My Daughter's Kitchen Table," also from *The Crack in Everything*, is a poem that shows Ostriker's strong, dogged intellect, and her ability to unite rawness and erudition. The poem's title promises something fairly conventional. Yet the wild, penetrating trajectory of the poem turns out to be more like Emerson than Elizabeth Bishop. It offers a layered, extended conceptual study:

> So in contrast with the intensity of the hard
> Buds, pulling themselves open,
> And on the other hand the grief
> Of the flabby dying leaves, comes the unconscious
> Soaring blossoms' thickened glory
> —Consciousness driving itself until it yields
> Narcosis of full being, the golden blossoms
> The petals of unconsciousness, which in turn break down
> At the advent of decay
> The very cells break down
> Into thought, curling,
> Gloomily ironic—
> The very cells break down, their membranes crushed
> And are dragged, as to a prison

Where the condemned
Beg for forgetfulness
Where the guards
Revel in brutality

What I admire in the extended performance of "Still Life"—of which the above is just an excerpt—is the doggedness of its conceptual description. The shrewd analysis of the growing plant in the vocabulary of the psyche would be ambitious all by itself; but in "Still Life," the poet presses abstraction past the point of conceptual convenience, into a brutal account of decomposition, the "degradation" of the organic return to matter. The ecstatic capaciousness of vision here is fine, but it is the final subjective turn in this passage that especially wows me, in which decay is characterized as a kind of humiliation, embodied in the strange, original metaphor of imprisonment and punishment: "the very cells break down, their membranes crushed / And are dragged, as to a prison // Where the condemned / Beg for forgiveness / Where the guards / Revel in brutality." With its unconventional declaration of the personal offensiveness of death, that strange and resonant imagery feels both intimately individual and archetypal.

"Still Life" bears Ostriker's characteristic fingerprints—joining intellectual muscle to an astute archetypal intelligence—for what else is this image of death but a mythical representation of the underworld as a kind of torturer's dungeon? Often elsewhere, spiritual Judaism is an informing resource for Ostriker's vision, but inside *these* images is a pagan imagination that might have come from the *Iliad*. "Still Life" also demonstrates what this lunging homespun lineation is good for, when well-employed—it captures the electrical velocity and irregularity of perception and thinking itself. The mode may be plain, but the imagination underlying the poem is strange and sophisticated.

All of Ostriker's collections are *strong*, but as one reads the work chronologically, the profile of her instincts and talents becomes clearer. Ostriker's recent books, *The Book of Seventy* and *The Old Woman, the Tulip, and the Dog*, register the emergence of a more economical and fully integrated poet, one whose work contains less complaint about the world and more mythic contemplativeness. At the same time, the poetry's intensity and vigor is undiminished. A lifetime of channeling her diverse and dialectical preoccupations has made her comprehension into a natural force, which joins clarity with imagination. Often deceptively spare, the poems are richly complex, and as passionate as ever. A sensibility that can both harangue and praise, that can combine declaration and introspection with such effectiveness, is rare.

It sounds clichéd to say that a particular poet writes in a "fully human" voice—doesn't all poetry give voice to the fullness of humanness? (Well—no.) And aren't there a lot of different sounds, bandwidths, and styles of "humanness"? Undeniably. But Ostriker has managed to catch a pretty substantial portion of the human experience that matters, and has caught it in a taut lyric of contemporary American idiom, one that neither has its nose in the air nor dumbs down the contradictions and infarctions of living in our era. One of the things I most admire in the work is not just its comprehensiveness, but its compression—its deft, economical formulations of the most dire contradictions of the human condition.

The poignant and ruthless poem "Prayer in Autumn" is both an ars poetica and a self-confrontation, in which the poet examines the context and marrow of the artist's life. Here is the first third of the poem:

> As to the deep ineradicable flaws
> in the workmanship
>
> anger and envy
> anger and envy
>
> stemming from overenthusiasm
> that rises like a water lily from mud
>
> and the stone
> of self, of ego
>
> that insists on its imperial monologue
> that strangles its audience
>
> I would like to repent but I cannot
> I am ridden like a horse

In this closing metaphor, several intellectual systems—the Freudian, the shamanic, and the ecstatic—are braided into each other, as if the speaker is shape-shifting between parallel theological dimensions. Later in the same poem a still different (more vertically positioned) divinity is invoked: "We are not competent to make our vows / we are truly sorry // we pull you down from a cloud / or bend our knees to you like sideshow dogs." The tonal complexity that combines sincere supplication with self-implicating satire is another deft compression of the mature Ostriker.

The recent *The Old Woman, the Tulip, and the Dog* is Ostriker's most joyful collection. The ingenuity of the book's structural conceit is both simple and virtuosic; each poem consists of three stanzas, consecutively spoken by three representatives of earthly life: an old woman, a tulip, and a dog. Basic as this sounds, the poem-by-poem recombinations of meaning and feeling are full of offhand revelations, and part of the pleasure of these poems is their sense of improvisatory play and discovery. Here is the poem "In Every Life":

In every life there's a moment or two
when we disappear, the cruel wound
takes over, and then again
at times we are filled with trees
or with birds
or with polishing the furniture
said the old woman

I know what you mean said the tulip
about epiphanies
for instance a breezy April day
the approach of a butterfly
but as to the disappearing self
no
I have not yet experienced that

You are creating distinctions
that do not exist in nature
where "self" and "not-self" are like salt
in ocean, cloud in sky
oxygen in fire
said the philosophical dog
under the table scratching his balls

In this collection, the dividends of age and technical fluency are visible. No longer compelled by the adamant pursuit of an absolute truth, the speaker of the poems seems to have relaxed into the comfortable cosmic milieu of multiple perspectives. The whole collection is as un-self-important and offhandedly profound as the example above. None of Ostriker's themes are left behind, though we could say that the sphere of concerns has been distilled to quintessential human matters—mortality, beauty, endurance, time, purpose—all handled lightly while retaining substance. What emerges more and more in Ostriker's work is a fluid dexterity. Here is another three-stanza poem, "In War Time," which displays the same pleasures of tonal quickness, invention, sobriety, and surprise:

> Ah here you are at last
> sorry about the guards
> I hope they didn't give you too much trouble
> I was afraid you'd never make it
> across the river before curfew
> let me take your coats
> said the old woman
>
> Thank you
> how could we possibly pass up
> such a sweet invitation
> but let me tell you
> said the tulip
> when we reached the bridge we saw
> the river was full of corpses
>
> A dog too can be afraid
> despite an appearance of ferocity
> navigating unfamiliar streets
> dodging unpredictable explosions
> still one persists in one's errand
> here we are said the dog
> thank you I will keep my coat.

There are many aspects of Ostriker's talent that deserve more praise—her erotic spirituality, for example, is uniquely refreshing. But let me end by emphasizing one other verifying element in her work: the speaker's recurring assertion of pride in humanness. We might well ask ourselves why such declarations should be so rare in our poetry, but they are as scarce as unicorns. Ostriker's speaker sings of her endurance, her vitality and accomplishment: ". . . I am like a swimmer," she says, in the poem "Heaven," "easily floating beyond where the surf breaks // my mind is a cervix / I can imagine anything." Elsewhere she concludes "West Fourth Street" proudly, "I have learned to be a fool for beauty." In these late poems, especially, the mature poet has found the sure channel of her force and her dexterity; it feels like the fluency for which a lifelong artist strives, where method and meaning come together with no accompanying loss of complexity.

I began this essay talking about luck, timing, and the mechanics of cultural recognition. Still another instance bears mentioning. Ostriker in her seventies and eighties, a survivor of a dozen American culture wars, and a witness to many stages of empire and generational change, is writing some of the best distinctive poems of her life. As an older woman poet, she is also in a category of near cultural invisibility—what are the chances that her excellence will be recognized? Such things may be out of our hands. Yet to me, Ostriker is an American poet of singular scope and force, one who at various times reminds me of W. S. Merwin, and at times of Anna Swir, or Wisława Szymborska. One can only say, go and see for yourself; begin anywhere. Here is a poet of the real stuff, and one for our time, fully human, keen, ruthless and merciful, fully rewarding to read.

JULIE R. ENSZER

"Climb the tree, / Be the tree, / Burn like that"

Judy Grahn, Alicia Ostriker,
and "the Shock of Pleasure"

I.

The life spills over, some days.
She cannot be at rest,
Wishes she could explode

Like that red tree—
The one that bursts into fire
All this week.[1]

I saw a red tree burst into fire. At a conference on women's poetry in Brooklyn. Organized by Wendy Galgan, the conference was, in part, an homage to the women who mentored Galgan during her PhD studies at the City University of New York. Alicia Ostriker spoke and read from her poetry. I confess, by the time Ostriker took the podium, I was tired. It was afternoon. We had been sitting in an auditorium a good part of the day. Although as a graduate student I have been trained for such marathon sitting and thinking sessions, my energy and attention were flagging. My mind was wandering; it would not rest. The magical, electrifying moment, the moment of flames, happened when Ostriker read from the work of Judy Grahn. Ostriker read "She Who." Boldly. Aggressively. Tenderly. "She Who" is not an easy poem to read aloud. The poem consists entirely of the two words in the title. Grahn animates the poem on the page with capitalization, punctuation, and spacing. Ostriker transformed Grahn's typography into a sonic salvo. Her rendering of "She Who" from the page to our ears was invigorating. After hearing Ostriker read "She Who" and talk about Grahn's work, I was changed. I had the capacity for deeper understanding and appreciation. My mind exploded. My body burst into fire. I carried that feeling with me for an entire week.

Ostriker describes Grahn's collection, *She Who*, as a chant and a quest "for an integrated female self" that is "inseparable from linguistic revolution."[2] One of the revolutionary components of *She Who* is how Grahn reconfigures relationships between and among women. Grahn resists the traditional generational constructs of grandmother, mother, and daughter, and the conflicts they engender, to posit new forms of relational communality for women.[3] The two plainsongs in the collection, "Slowly: a plainsong from an older woman to a younger woman" and "a funeral: plainsong from a younger woman to an older woman," in particular reimagine relationships between women.

"Slowly" is an incantatory poem about age, the past, and the relationship of both to the present. The poem begins "am I not olden olden olden[.]" The archaic, adjectival form of old, olden, sets the controlling consonant sound, *n*, for the first half of the poem. The *n*s cascade down the page—"wanting," "broken," "common," "ridden," "version"—providing sonic unity. The sound of the *n* is punctuated by additional internal rhyme. Grahn weaves rhyme with long, open vowels such as the long *a*s in the fourth stanza: "aged," "shake," "glazing," "hazy," and "craven." Grahn contrasts the assonance with hard consonant sounds from the third stanza: "crinkled," "cranky," "glinty." The concatenation of assonance and consonance in the poem creates a highly stylized diction for the speaker. Grahn voices the older woman with a full soundscape—making puns, rhyming words, and layering vowels and consonants. The density of the speaker's diction suggests the richness of her experience and invites readers to consider the progression of age as equally rich and dense.

A series of caesuras, created through the addition of space between words within lines, complements the sonic density and slows the eye's progress down the page, particularly in later print editions of the work that utilize a more conventional typography. Through the caesuras, Grahn invites breaks in reading and introduces breaks for the speaker. These pauses are thoughtful, never forgetful, and build anticipation for what is to come.

From the poem's subtitle, readers know that the poem is spoken by an older woman to a younger woman. The speaker slyly embraces and refuses age. In the first line she asks, "am I not olden," but then quickly refutes it in the second line, "it is unwanted." This opening couplet suggests both the inevitability of the passage of time—the speaker asks, am I old?—and the resistance to time's passing when the speaker asserts, it is unwanted.

The indeterminacy of the two women—named only as "older" and "younger"—invites readers to consider them as individuals and as metonymic for larger groups of women. The speaker acknowledges tension between herself and the younger woman—as individuals and as members of a group. The speaker voices conflict in the climax of the poem. She says, "do you not turn away your shoulder? / have I not shut my mouth against you?" Initially, the hostilities expressed are through slights, physical and verbal, yet they capture profound pain. The speaker continues with the sharpest rebuke of the poem: "are you not shamed to treat me meanly / when you discover you become me?" This withering question is tempered by the next line, "are you not proud that you become me?" Grahn's plainsong does not punish the younger woman, though she speaks to demand accountability. The emotional complexity in the relationship between the older woman and the younger woman resists flattening or caricaturing either of them. At the same time, the speaker recognizes and implicates herself in the conflicts between women. Grahn grapples with generational conflict and affirms the inevitability of aging and generations: we all become older.

In the next stanza, the older woman unites with the younger woman, telling her, "I will not shut my mouth against you. / do not turn away your shoulder." The speaker imagines a shared and reciprocal relationship between the two. She acknowledges that both women "brew in the same bitters / that boil us away" and concludes, "we both need stronger water." This is the revolutionary vision that Grahn proffers: women of all ages working together to create a different world.

One project of the speaker in "Slowly" is to acknowledge her age and the experience of age, but also to engage the younger woman, the listener, and ultimately the reader to join her for a revolution. The poem concludes with the monostich, "are we not olden, olden, olden[.]" In this final stanza, the speaker repeats the first line of the poem with one key alteration: she replaces the singular subject in the first line of the poem with the first-person plural subject in the final line. This implicates the younger woman and the reader in a shared generational location. The conclusion, without punctuation, either a period or a question mark, demonstrates how the speaker, listener, and reader are bound together in the world. At the conclusion of the poem, the plainsong comes to rest, but it is work that does not end. Ostriker's poem continues:

Senses her infinite smallness
But can't seize it,
Recognizes the folly of desire,

The folly of withdrawal—
Kicks at the curb, the pavement,
If only she could, at this moment,

When what she's doing is plodding
To the bus stop, to go to school,
Passing that fiery tree—if only she could

I first read *Stealing the Language* in 1988 or 1989, when an undergraduate at the University of Michigan. Encountering Ostriker on the page was another burning sensation. My copy is scribbled with notes: underlining, small check marks, stars. Each chapter has a handwritten summary in the white space on the final page. "Yes" is written next to many sentences, and "more." The folly of my desire. More thinking, more writing, more poems.

Ostriker articulated what has become my core value as a feminist critic. She wrote, I "believe that there exists a body of poetry by women which illuminates the condition of women and therefore of humanity in an unprecedented way, and which is exciting enough as poetry, as art, not merely to be accepted into the literary mainstream but to influence the stream's course."[4] Ostriker connects inductively that the condition of women is related to the condition of humanity; she affirms that poetry by women, particularly poetry that expresses the hopes and dreams of feminists throughout the twentieth century, should not only be in the literary mainstream but also influence its course. Ostriker concluded her introduction, "I hope . . . that the shock of pleasure at seeing something beautifully said will occur again and again to my readers as it has to me, and that they will be drawn into further investigation of these poets and poems."[5] Ostriker captured my own experience of *Stealing the Language*: the shock of pleasure—and the desire to investigate further. At the end of *Stealing the Language*, I wrote, "This is the kind of book that I want to write when I go to graduate school." *When* I go to graduate school. The certainty of my younger, teenaged self, the folly of my desire, still makes me smile. For sixteen years, feeling my infinite smallness, I plodded from work to home to work to home. Every time I moved, I unpacked *Stealing the Language*, put it in a special place on my bookshelf, thinking to myself, if only I could. If only I could. For nearly two decades, *Stealing the Language* was my fiery tree.

"A funeral" employs the incantatory style of both "Slowly" and of the other poems in *She Who*. In "a funeral," a younger woman is the speaker, addressing an older woman who has died. She begins, "I will be your mouth now, to do your singing." In this opening, Grahn defines a shared humanity between the two women, a realization of the bond between the two from the previous poem.

In the second stanza, the younger woman says, "the bond between women is a circle / we are together within it." Grahn develops this idea further near the conclusion of the poem when she writes,

> tell all the voices who speak to younger women
> tell all the voices who speak to us when we need it
> that the love between women is a circle
> and is not finished

This configuration of the relationships among women as circular subverts traditional assignations of age and gender. Grahn presents relationships among women not in the daughter, mother, grandmother matrix, or even in the maiden, mother, and crone matrix, but as women bound together in a circle. They may have different ages but these differences do not result in circumscribed roles. Grahn describes fluidity among women in their relationships with one another and even between their bodies in this world and the next. Part of how Grahn achieves this vision in "a funeral" is by rewriting liturgical texts.

A plainsong is a chant for a single voice. Invoking a musical intonation that rises and falls, Grahn weaves the sonority throughout the poem. The word *plainsong*, in addition to suggesting musicality, also invokes religion. Plainsongs were liturgical music. In both of these plainsongs, Grahn creates a new feminist liturgy, rooted in one traditional moment of liturgy, the funeral, but also honoring the daily experiences of life.

Liturgy is a conversation between people and G-d (the divine), often mediated by anointed religious leaders. Grahn reconfigures liturgy, however, as a conversation between women. The divine comes from the spark of commonality and communality among women. For Grahn, and for Ostriker, liturgy focuses less on dialogue with the divine and more on conversations between women. The divine emerges within women's relationships, unmediated by religion or religious leaders. Women, speaking together, access the divine with one another.

To create this feminist liturgy, Grahn generates lists that unfold within lines and stanzas. Consider this passage:

love of my love, I am your breast
arm of my arm, I am your strength
breath of my breath, I am your foot
thigh of my thigh, back of my back
eye of my eye, beat of my beat
kind of my kind, I am your best

The melding of the two women's bodies through the language of the speaker binds them together. The lines echo the book of Ruth where Ruth says, "Entreat me not to leave thee, and to return from following after thee; for whither thou goest, I will go; and where thou lodgest, I will lodge; thy people shall be my people."[6] Grahn recaps this rhetorical structure later in the poem:

want of my want, I am your lust
wave of my wave, I am your crest
earth of my earth, I am your crust
may of my may, I am your must
kind of my kind, I am your best

Although the poem is titled "a funeral" and Grahn labels it "for ritual use only,"[7] the liturgical elements of the poem come from both funeral liturgies and marriage rites. By doing this, Grahn returns to the circular images she invoked earlier for women's relationships—"love between women is a circle / and is not finished[.]" Similarly, women's lives are circular:

a mountain when it is no longer
a mountain, goes to the sea
when the sea dies it goes to the rain

when the rain dies it goes to the grain
when the grain dies it goes to the flesh
when the flesh dies it goes to the mountain

This circular or periodic return to life is the ideology Grahn enacts.
The lack of completion, the sense of a life with no end, is the con-
solation Grahn offers in this poem.

In the final two stanzas of the poem, Grahn writes:

you have put your breath upon mine
I shall wrap my entire fist around you
I can touch any woman's lip to remember

we are together in my motion
you have wished us a bonded life

Grahn combines the breath / life imagery that is conventionally
associated with funerals with the fist, a sign of power, rebellion, and
resistance. She affirms as the younger woman speaker that "we are
together," we, the younger woman and the older woman, have "a
bonded life." Grahn acknowledges the structures in which we orga-
nize generational relationships, but she resists them, offering instead
new imagery and new modes of thinking about relationships be-
tween and among women through the creation of a feminist liturgy.

. . . —if only she could

Be making love,
Be making poetry,
Be exploding, be speeding through the universe

Like a photon, like a shower
Of yellow blazes—
She believes if she could only overtake

The riding rhythm of things, of her own electrons,
Then she would be at rest—
If she could forget school,

I forgot school. I forgot my convictions to write a book like
Stealing the Language. When I was twenty years old in 1990, all I
wanted to write about was contemporary lesbian poetics. I fancied
this an excellent dissertation topic, one inspired by *Stealing the Lan-*

guage, but also by the lesbian poetry published throughout the 1970s and 1980s. Perhaps the only book more dog-eared than *Stealing the Language* was Marilyn Hacker's *Love, Death, and the Changing of the Seasons.* In spite of the flowering of feminist literary criticism when I was an undergraduate and the opportunities it presented for feminist scholars, responses to my desire to write about contemporary lesbian poetics were tepid. Professors suggested I focus my academic desires on the early modern period; they said there was much work to be done on early modern women writers, and a stronger job market. Graduate schools rejected me. In retrospect, I understand these rejections as a consequence of two things: my tender age and my passion for political work. Perhaps people recognized I needed to cut my teeth working in community-based organizations before returning to the university. I did just that. It took me a long time to return. When I started graduate school in 2006, much had changed, though my passion for writing about contemporary lesbian poetics still encountered some dubious responses. At one particularly low point during my MFA, I emailed my best friend, "Really, my last hope is Martha Nell Smith. If she doesn't like my work, no one will." Typing those words, I did not realize that Ostriker's influence, not only on the page, was destined to be part of my graduate education.

Climb the tree,
Be the tree,
Burn like that.

II.

She doesn't know yet, how could she,
That this same need
Is going to erupt every September

And that in fifty years the idea will hit her
For no apparent reason, in a laundromat
Between a washer and a dryer,

Like one of those electric bulbs
Suddenly lighting up in comic strips—
There in that naked and soiled place

With its detergent machines,
Its speckled fluorescent lights,
Its lint piles broomed into corners, . . .

Grahn's plainsongs locate themselves in philosophical and sacred spaces as the source of the philosophical and sacred. Ostriker's "A Young Woman, a Tree" relishes the quotidian.[8] It is tripartite, the three sections almost echoing the generational configuration of daughter, mother, grandmother. Yet like Grahn, Ostriker resists these generational configurations. Ostriker contains the passage of time within a single woman's life. Like Grahn, she connects women's life cycle with nature, in particular, the life cycle of a tree.

The first section of "A Young Woman, a Tree" maps the desire to move away from daily life into a more rarefied space with explosions of color, sexuality, and creativity. It concludes with the poet's direct address to "Climb the tree, / Be the tree, / Burn like that." In the second section, Ostriker tempers her exuberant command with a vision of how the sacred enters daily life. The second stanza opens in a laundromat. The young woman, previously desiring to speed through the universe "like a photon, like a shower / of yellow blazes—" now finds herself, fifty years later, in the most ordinary of places, "naked and soiled," promising cleanliness amid the "lint piles broomed into corners."

Like Grahn's articulation of the unity of desires between the older woman and the younger woman, Ostriker writes that the young woman has "this same need . . . erupt every September[.]" The need for a spectacular explosion, for a life lived at high velocity, for combustion. This desire, represented by the image of the burning tree, is a life force present in the young woman and the woman fifty years later. Through the life of one woman, Ostriker refutes narratives about generations that separate young women from old women.

As she fumbles for quarters
And dimes, she will double over
Into the plastic basket's

Mountain of wet
Bedsheets and bulky overalls—
Old lady! She'll grin at herself,

Old lady! The desire
To burn is already a burning!
How about that!

The other graduate students in my program are discontent. We don't earn enough money. We have to work other jobs; outside work means that we can't complete our benchmarks in a timely fashion. We will never finish. We will never get jobs. This is the dirge of graduate school. There is nothing poetic about it. No desire to burn. No burning.

One faculty member called us apprentices; the term makes my graduate student counterparts chafe. They want to be seen as colleagues, as future peers, or as employees, entitled to adequate compensation, healthcare, workplace protections. My department changes its nomenclature for faculty members from *advisors* to *mentors*. They hope that the term *mentor* will open space for collegial relations between graduate students and faculty members. I don't care about any of this. I want everyone to leave me alone. I want to sit in front of my computer. I want to burn.

When I worked for nonprofits, I never negotiated for titles, only money. I told people, I don't care what you call me, I only care what is in my paycheck. I still don't care what you call me. I only care what is in my mind. What I imagine I will write tomorrow.

I am an apprentice to many, living and dead—Bishop, Rukeyser, Hacker, Rich. I want to be an apprentice to great women poets until I die. At every age, I want to study the craft of language; I want to labor with beautiful words; I want to create meaning with images. I want to burn.

The desire to burn is already a burning.

III.

Meanwhile the maple
Has also survived, and thinks
It owes its longevity

To its location
Between a bus stop
And a bar, and to its uniquely

Mutant appetite for pollutants:
Carbon monoxide, alcohol, spit. . . .
The truth is, it enjoys city life.

While the tripartite structure of "A Young Woman, a Tree" resists allusions to the different phases of womanhood, it lends itself to the rhetorical structure of thesis, antithesis, and synthesis. In the first section, Ostriker offers the thesis of the burning desire for creative expression using the metaphor of the changing color of the fiery tree. In the second section, Ostriker demonstrates the antithesis, that the need for creative expression, for a fiery engagement with the world, is not exclusive to the younger woman; the woman has the same desire fifty years later. The third section offers the synthesis of these two through the personification of the maple, "that red tree." The synthesis is a philosophical transformation, enacted with the metaphor of a tree. The magic that infused the tree in the mind of the young woman changes in the second section. The physical location of the tree, near a bus stop and a bar, and the observation about its "mutant appetite for pollutants" reveal the quotidian life of the tree.

Ostriker confides the inner fantasies of the tree in the same way she confided the fantasies of the young woman in the first section of the poem. She then presents the real answer. Nothing highbrow; rather, simply, the tree "enjoys city life." It enjoys being where it is planted. It possesses a wisdom we readers might wish for the young woman.

Regular working people suffer so harshly
It makes a tree feel happier,
Having nothing to do

But feel its thousand orgasms each spring
Or stretch its limbs during the windy days
That are like a Swedish massage,

Or swoon into the fall
Among its delicious rain-patters,
Its saffron and red glowings.

Then, when the tethered leaves
Snatch themselves away like desperate
Children ardent for freedom,

It will let itself sigh, feel wise
and resigned, and draw
Its thoughts downward to its other crown,

Contrasting the life of the tree to "regular working people," Ostriker considers periodicity through the life of the tree. The year is linked to carnal experiences that map obliquely to women's lives—spring orgasms, Swedish massages, fall swoonings. The loss of leaves at the beginning of winter is likened to "adolescents ardent for freedom." In winter, the tree looks "downward to its other crown." The wisdom of the tree is in the roots—"the secret leafless system." For Ostriker, the question isn't of generations, which proceed linearly, but of periodicity, a measurement of time that continually returns. *Generations* suggests a progressive narrative in which forward progress equals loss of the past.[9] Seasons return. The periodicity that Ostriker invokes operates in a similar register with the circularity that Grahn envisions. For Ostriker, the relationship of periodicity suggests the continual possibility of return and the possibilities of conversations among women; for Grahn, circularity does this work.

The secret leafless system
That digs in dark
Its thick intelligent arms

And stubborn hands
Under the shops, the streets,
The subways, the granite,

The sewage pipes'
Cold slime,
As deep as that.

While my peers worry about mentorship, where to find it, what it should look like, what to call it, I have found a "secret leafless system / that digs in dark." I, like the younger woman in Grahn's poem, "Slowly," learn by listening. I learn by reading. Martha Nell Smith liked my work enough to become codirector of my dissertation. Ostriker directed Smith's dissertation on Emily Dickinson twenty-five years earlier. This could be a story of generations, but like these poems by Grahn and Ostriker, I resist.

This is what I learned from Martha: attend to the text. Consider publishing practices. Turn off email. Do your own work. Don't apologize. Be bold. Be generous. Be kind. What you discover writing your dissertation you will still be thinking about, writing about, twenty-five years later. These lessons are independent of the name the department, the university, gives her.

This is what I learned from Alicia: Read deeply and eclectically. Create space for the sacred and the profane. Have visionary opinions and defend them ferociously. Listen to other ways of knowing. Work inductively. Write poetry, write criticism. Burn like that. Retire. Continue to publish books every two years.

The output is the fiery red tree. The book, bound. The course, complete. The secret is the leafless system, digging in darkness. In graduate school, the product is in the process. The hours of thinking and writing. The solitude. We yearn for the fire, for the limbs massaging the sky, but the secret is in the other crown. The gift of mentors is to glance at the "thick intelligent arms // And stubborn hands" working daily in cold slime. Look at the tree between the bus stop and the bar, but remember the secret leafless system. It is as deep as that.

Am I the young woman? The tree? The plainsong?

I locate myself not in conventional systems of generations but in textual practices. I locate my intellectual attentions in the past and present models of Alicia Ostriker and Martha Nell Smith. In the palimpsest of Judy Grahn, Emily Dickinson, Muriel Rukeyser, and a raft of other women poets. I attend to words and to modes of publishing. Grahn's two plainsongs and Ostriker's "A Young Woman, a Tree" imagine circular, or periodic, relationships among women. Both poets create a new feminist liturgy for expressing and celebrating women's lives. Both poets burn with the shock of pleasure. Both poets weave with red thread. Connecting our lives. Drawing us into a circle.

> *are we not olden   olden olden*
> *Be the tree,*
> *Burn like that.*

Notes

1. From "A Young Woman, a Tree," pp. 331–34 in *Poetry* 150.6 (September 1987). I quote this poem in its entirety throughout the essay at the beginning and end of sections. The text printed here is the text originally presented in *Poetry*; Ostriker made minor revisions for its inclusion in *Green Age*.

2. Ostriker, *Stealing the Language*, 202.

3. Feminist history grapples with generational constructs and conflicts extensively. Nancy Whittier's *Feminist Generations: The Persistence of the Radical Women's Movement* (Philadelphia: Temple University Press, 1995) examines how the point of politicization shapes generational thinking. Recently, feminist historians have reconsidered the "wave" metaphor for feminism in a series of essays in *No Permanent Waves: Recasting Histories of U.S. Feminism*, edited by Nancy A. Hewitt (New Brunswick, NJ: Rutgers University Press, 2010). Finally, Susan Faludi's article "American Electra: Feminism's Ritual Matricide" in *Harpers* (October 2010: 29–42) demonstrates how conflict within feminism can be understood through a generational lens. This essay reframes generations within feminism using Grahn and Ostriker's poetry.

4. Ostriker, *Stealing the Language*, 13.

5. Ibid., 14.

6. Book of Ruth, chapter 1, verse 16, Jewish Publication Service.

7. In *The Work of a Common Woman*, Grahn writes that this plainsong "is not a poem at all, it is a funeral ritual, and has been used at memorials a number of times" (*Common Woman*, 76).

8. Ostriker, of course, doesn't avoid the philosophical or the sacred in her work. She grapples keenly with these questions in other poems and in her critical work *For the Love of God: The Bible as an Open Book* (New Brunswick, NJ: Rutgers University Press, 2009) and *Feminist Revision and the Bible: The Unwritten Volume* (Hoboken, NJ: Wiley-Blackwell, 1993).

9. The term *generations* also suggests a narrative that reproduces heterosexuality. Recently, this narrative has been extensively critiqued by scholars such as Judith Halberstam in *In a Queer Time and Place*, where she describes "queer time" that "disrupts conventional accounts of youth culture, adulthood, and maturity" (New York: New York University Press, 2005, 2); Lee Edelman in *No Future*, where "queerness names the side of those not 'fighting for the children'" and a politics that resists "the absolute value of reproductive futurism" (Durham, NC: Duke University Press, 2004, 3); and David Eng in *The Feeling of Kinship*, which examines how gays and lesbians occupy "the normative structures of family and kinship" increasingly in a form of queer liberalism that "abets the forgetting of race" and denies racial difference (Durham, NC: Duke University Press, 2010, 3–4). These contemporary queer critiques of generations resonate with earlier feminist critiques and with the poetry of both Ostriker and Grahn.

ERIC SELINGER

Mixed Dancing

What is it to be a Jewish poet? What is it to be a Jewish woman poet? I did not always ask these questions.
—ALICIA OSTRIKER, PREFACE TO THE BOOK OF LIFE: SELECTED JEWISH POEMS, 1979–2011

"*I am and am not a Jew,*" Ostriker declares in the opening sentence of *The Nakedness of the Fathers* (1994), the collection of essays and poems—her first midrashic efforts, wobbly as colts—that marked her emergence as a Jewish feminist author. Her reputation as a feminist tout court was already solid, thanks to a pair of critical studies, *Writing Like a Woman* (essays on H.D., Plath, Sexton, Swenson, and Rich) and *Stealing the Language: The Emergence of Women's Poetry in America*, along with seven books of restless, politically charged poems exploring marriage, pregnancy, motherhood, and the female artist's calling. Long before she was and was not a Jew, Ostriker was and was not a wife, a lover, a mother, writing a divided, argumentative poetry derived in part from her "confrontational and adversarial inclinations," as she calls them in *Nakedness*, and in part from her "hero and guru" William Blake, who taught her that "without contraries is no progression" and "opposition is true friendship."

"*They say a Jew is somebody who loves to argue, especially with God and other Jews,*" Ostriker writes in *Nakedness*. Should we call these early poems "Jewish," then? I could make the case that their argumentative quality links them with a Jewish taste for "disputation without telos," in Daniel Boyarin's phrase. Ostriker's essay on Ginsberg, written as she began, in the early 1990s, to "wrestle with issues of spirituality in general and what Judaism signifies to me in particular," gives us more compelling terms to work with. "*Howl* Revisited: The Poet as Jew" teases out the filial, bodily tenderness of the older poet as his echt Judaic quality, right up there with his itch to write a latter-day book of Lamentations. We might call this a

---

A version of this essay appeared in *Parnassus* 34, nos. 1 & 2 (2015): 377–408.

"carnal" Jewishness, following Boyarin, or even a "turbulent, fleshy, sensual" one, since it braids Ginsberg's qualities of "Yiddish kindness" and "Hebraic prophecy" with a Whitmanian sense that America is a land of "infinite hope and infinite disappointment." Not that this last isn't also "very Jewish," Ostriker explains; think of Yip Harburg, lyricist both of "Somewhere Over the Rainbow" and "Brother, Can You Spare a Dime?"

In his entry on Jewish-American poetry for the *Encyclopedia Judaica*, poet-critic Norman Finkelstein praises *The Nakedness of the Fathers* as Ostriker's "boldest venture into midrash," a book where "poetry and prose, narrative and hermeneutic, personal reflection and scholarly exegesis are combined in a remarkably comprehensive reconsideration of nearly all the major tales and figures in the Torah." The scope of the book is bold and the mix of genres refreshing—"it resembles the Bible, the original multi-genre experiment," Ostriker modestly notes in her essay "Secular and Sacred: Returning (to) the Repressed." Some of poetry in it may or may not have been automatic writing, such as "The Opinion of Hagar" and "The Opinion of Aaron," as well as some of Ostriker's exegetical moves.

The strength of *Nakedness* lies, for me, in its autobiographical material and the erotic gusto with which Ostriker stakes her claims to tradition and scripture. They're "mine," she writes, and in fact she uses that key word throughout the book. It first shows up in in this primal scene:

> *I pull the chenille spread from my bed, wrap it around myself for a cloak, tiptoe through the darkness to my parents' room, and push open the door. What strikes my senses first is an odor new to me: pungent, briny, and sweet. In an instant my eyes can already make out my mother and father moving under their blanket, hugging tightly, and something in my head is already shouting Mine! Mine!*

Traces of a lost matriarchal past in the Bible are also "mine," she writes a few pages later. Down the page, "*the Torah is / My well of living waters / Mine.*" Later, as Adam and Eve begin to play games of flirtation and companionship, Ostriker slips in to paraphrase the Song of Songs: "My beloved is mine and I am hers / We are feeding among the lilies." Learning cursive, the young Ostriker struggles to write the capital letter of her first name on "*clean smooth paper*" which "*emanates potency. Mine, mine!*" Access to Torah here means access to the father as erotic object and to the daughter's power to choose or deny him: "Mine—here—in Vision—and in Veto!" as Emily Dickinson's poem "Mine—by the Right of / the White Election!" triumphantly claims. And what does her mother say to all of this? In my favorite moment in the book, the young Ostriker asks if she can marry daddy when she grows up. Her mother doesn't bat an eye, the poet reports, assuring her that she can—"*If I still want to.*"

As *Nakedness* ends, Ostriker's focus shifts from the self-mythologizing to the more purely mythic. The book closes with a wry parable in which God the Father turns out to be not dead but pregnant and in labor, followed by Ostriker's "Prayer to the Shekhinah" as a rousing recessional hymn. (*Shekinah* is a grammatically feminine term for the imminent Presence of God.) The real conclusion of the book, though, comes just before, in an essay called "Tree of Life," in which Ostriker has an exchange with a woman who's looking for a Biblical quote for her mother's gravestone—something other than the "woman of valor" bit from Proverbs. "*There must be some biblical women who do something besides being housewives*," the friend growls, and Ostriker reels them off, from Huldah the prophet (2 Kings 22) to Wisdom and the Shekhinah and the (again, grammatically feminine) Torah herself, the Tree of Life to those who hold fast to her. "*My friend is a working woman*," the essay ends. "*She leads a busy life and has very little patience for metaphysical speculation. So far as she is concerned, whether there is a God or there is not a God, a Shekhinah or not a Shekhinah, you still have to fight City Hall. [. . .] When I suggest that she could use the tree of life quote for her mother's stone, she says she will think about it.*" That's the kind of skeptical, open-ended cadence that the book deserves. The writer's block that Ostriker hit after publishing *Nakedness* suggests that she, too, knew on some level that she'd gone astray, sacrificing snark and disputation, two of her greatest gifts, on the altar of She Who.

Nothing, My Lord

"When I finished *Nakedness*," Ostriker explained in "Secular and Sacred,"

> I thought the next thing I needed to do was have a goddess-vision: to imagine her body would mean to help bring her forth

into the world. I read volumes of women's spirituality, most of which were too sweet for my taste. I read Gershom Scholem, Raphael Patai, and Daniel Matt's beautiful translation of the Zohar. I read H.D., Denise Levertov, Anne Sexton (not the "confessional" poems but the *Psalms* and *The Awful Rowing Toward God*), Lucille Clifton. To each of these profoundly intelligent and profoundly spiritual women poets the goddess had, if only as a glimmer, appeared. I waited for her to appear to me.

Nothing happened. Nada. No vision. In fact, no poetry.

The chronology is tricky here. In point of fact, two books of poetry happened: *The Crack in Everything* (1996), its title taken from Leonard Cohen's "Anthem," and *The Little Space*, which followed two years later. Yet neither hints, in style or substance, at the year of aphoristic shards and fractured arguments that came to Ostriker from December 1998 through the following winter. In 2002 these were published as *the volcano sequence*: a signal achievement in Jewish-American poetry.

The clipped negations of Ostriker's essay—"Nothing happened"; "No vision"; "no poetry"—hint at the central paradox of *the volcano sequence*. In this book of poems that are often not quite poems, about visions that are anything but visionary, the word "nothing" shows up as often and crucially as "mine" does in *Nakedness*. "There is nothing but what is said," Samuel Beckett intones in the second of the book's four epigraphs, adding that, therefore, "Beyond what is said, there is nothing," and Ostriker's longing to bring that nothing from the unsaid into the spoken or written haunts and propels the sequence. At the simplest level, this is a home video of apophatic theology gone wild: That "nothing" is a God-name plucked from the "Homage to Rumi," where Ostriker tells God that "They say I should try calling you Nothing— / But I don't know / If I'm ready for that yet." By the end of the 1990s, she was ready, if only because she'd discovered how capacious and productive that name could be. After introducing "nothing" in the book's epigraphs, for example, she drops the word, or holds it back, for nearly twenty pages, using the space to introduce herself as a character ("I am like a volcano / that has blown itself / out of the water," prone to destroying those she loves with eruptions of "thick and magnificent rage"), and, through a disheartened expostulation, introducing the book's motif of an address to the deity. ("doomed either way, dear God," she writes to close one poem; turn the page, and she's realized that the expression wasn't just a sigh—it was an *epistolary* sigh, the start of a conversation, if only on the page.)

When does "nothing" return? In the book's first section, God gets addressed, described, brushed off, accused, and possibly channeled, since Ostriker's short, unpunctuated lines of estrangement and regret read equally well as spoken by either party. (Later, God's lines are set off in italics.) Ostriker then begins to hint at a context for this dialogue of one: a daughter-mother relationship that has likewise foundered. Suddenly the word crops up again. "Although I have put an ocean between us," she writes in "mother,"

> still do you know how I lie awake at night
> the eye in my right palm pictures you
> sitting amid your litter, feet buried
> by accumulated jars of buttons,
> glasses lost beneath a decade of bank statements
> and funny poems,
> hands folded under your chin, staring
> at nothing, preparing to be blind
> and helpless, for fifty years
> it has tortured me that I cannot save you from madness
> and that I do not love you enough
>
> what is enough
> nothing is enough

If "nothing" was already a code word for the God who is and is not there, then "God" is now also a code word, a name for what "enough love" would entail. Like the mad Naomi mourned in Ginsberg's "Kaddish," Ostriker's mother bodies forth the material world as a broken, wounded, wounding, unlovable thing: She is a "monologist, mistress of futility / . . . killing and saving, more or less at random, / beetles, roaches, flies, / writing illegible puzzles / dead fish crammed in your ceiling." To borrow a term from the book's first epigraph, "Lead me from the unreal to the real" (from the Upanishads), the poet's "mama / maya" stands for the "real," and all of the poet's grapplings with the "unreal" deity—a Shekhinah, a Man Behind the Curtain, an abstraction of "ruthless radiance"—are ultimately efforts to embrace her.

As in the best, most personal passages of *Nakedness*, where Biblical commentaries blossom from Ostriker's family romance, *the volcano sequence* sees its own subjects doubly. Every theological proposition is avowedly and self-consciously a psychological projection, the mother-daughter drama playing out on a cosmic scale; at the same time, the actual mother-daughter relationship plays out in a Jewish culture shaped, in no small part, by the exile of what Raphael Patai once dubbed "the Hebrew Goddess." ("my mother my queen / I was trying to catch you," Ostriker jots in a dream-poem, late in the book.) The doublings proliferate, as Ostriker composes both psalms and anti-psalms, weaves lines from American authors (Ralph Ellison and Malcom X, most notably) into paraphrased texts from the Biblical prophets, and hears an echo of scripture in the earliest words of a toddler. "You bring a future that is not my death," she tells God on the penultimate page: "like my grandchild I will learn / to say hello to say ball / to say go up." "Go up" is, of course, the final phrase of the Hebrew Bible, at least in English: "Thus saith Cyrus king of Persia, All the kingdoms of the earth hath the LORD God of heaven given me; and he hath charged me to build him a house in Jerusalem, which is in Judah. Who is there among you of all his people? The LORD his God be with him, and let him go up." And although Ostriker rarely indulges in puns elsewhere, *the volcano sequence* glitters with wordplay and double-entendres. "*It is your rhetoric that beguiles me*," God says in "addendum to Jonah," but if this feisty deity is eager for human beings to talk him out of destroying things, "*your word against / mine*," the torque of Ostriker's line break suggests that those human arguments are, themselves, being claimed as divine ("*your word against / [is] mine*"). And when she decides to call God "Being," she does so knowing that this is

a word with two contradictory
meanings   someone to wipe the blood
and dirty tears away through boundless love

someone able to punish listen wrestle
like a person but
larger

and *ein sof*   boundless
being   in the sense of pure existence   remote
abstraction more impersonal than zero

you exquisite
joke   you paradigm paradox
you absent presence   you good evil   shredding the eye

so that it can become a door

[. . .]

    you complete nothing

    you perfect nothing

Is "complete" an adjective or a verb? What about "perfect"? You can't say the latter out loud without choosing, since where you place accent determines the part of speech: a lovely instantiation of the "paradigm paradox" that Ostriker has in mind.

As Time Goes By

"I see myself / / as an aperture," Ostriker writes late in *the volcano sequence.* "Words pass through, addressing/imagining/inventing / One, of whom nothing is known that is not words." But "aperture" doesn't suffice for her character here. Wistful, ribald, theologically speculative, given to mordant political humor, she is a remarkable contribution to Jewish-American literature, though the neglect of the book by scholars suggests that they're troubled or embarrassed by the figure Ostriker presents. Perhaps she's just more intimate with her imagined Beloved than Jewish tradition, at least in America, tends to countenance. ("would you turn off that faucet, I shout to my husband / but to you I say: never turn it off.") The final section of the book, "The Space of This Dialogue," plays up Ostriker's carnality. Nearly half of the *volcano sequence* poems reproduced in *The Book of Life* are drawn from this section, as though it were the keynote not just of the book but of her entire Jewish imagination. She has no time, in her poems at least, for commandments and ritual, but the injunction to "choose life" (Deuteronomy 30:19), plucked out of context, goads and sustains her, giving Hebraic sanction for a love of the material world that would, in another poet, be Christological (Hopkins), syncretic Buddhist (Snyder), Romantic (Whitman, Keats), or simply secular (Williams, O'Hara).

In the closing lines of *the volcano sequence,* Ostriker notes that while "sometimes the stories take you and fling you against a wall," as in "A Meditation on Seven Days" and *The Nakedness of the Fathers,* the encounter with tradition isn't always so bruising. "sometimes you go right through the wall," the book ends. I've never cottoned to this as a closing couplet; the shift from "a" to "the" feels slight, and I can't do much with that repeated "wall." Yet the longer I live with the book, the more I savor this flatness as a deliberate gesture, as though Ostriker were refusing to end her sequence with a resonant, climactic cadence. Something more *ought* to happen, my ear reminds me: at the very least, another "sometimes" line to round out a threefold crescendo. Ostriker's subsequent writing fills that gap, bringing to light what she discovers on the far side of that wall, or what happens when it comes down.

Since *the volcano sequence*, she has published *For the Love of God* (2007), a book of essays on some of the "most unconventional and outrageous portions" of the Hebrew Bible, as well as four books of poetry: *No Heaven* (2005), *The Book of Seventy* (2009), *The Old Woman, the Tulip, and the Dog* (2014), and *Waiting for the Light* (2017). None of these returns to the stylistic experiments and theological speculations of *the volcano sequence*, but each bears the marks of that earlier sojourn. The essay "Psalm and Anti-Psalm" in *For the Love of God*, for example, grows out of the poems in both modes from *the volcano sequence*, and more generally from Ostriker's increasing comfort with engaging the "mixed god" she sees in a glass brightly, "with the veil of righteousness removed." It's a joy to hear her call out a former poet laureate for blithely espousing the Psalms as a source of consolation after 9/11, and to watch her smite Stephen Mitchell for his tidied-up version of Psalm 137, which cuts off halfway through. "Has New Age sentimental niceness claimed another victim?" Ostriker asks. "Is he trying to convert the Psalms to Buddhism? Is he trying to castrate God? Who does he think he's fooling?" In *No Heaven*, meanwhile, she returns to her first great subjects, marriage and sex, with a rueful, newfound ease, weaving slips of allusion from the Bible and popular culture into her texts just as she did when writing about the *odi-et-amo* tug of war between God and Jonah in the previous book. The end of "In the Forty-Fifth Year of Marriage" is a particularly fine example of this mode:

Marriage is that complicated, a house with living rooms and
    bedrooms,
And the usual basement and attic nobody likes to go to—
Horrible cobwebs in the basement, low rafters in the attic—

It is tough, that cord not easily broken
That sometimes seems a noose, but today I wished to speak
Of your beauty, bravely cresting in your sixties, at an age

When your parents were gone, an attractive hard-living
Man and woman, and perhaps they've lent your clay
Some excess excellence for me to appreciate

—*That I'll have to leave ere long. As time goes by. Silver threads among,*
For it's a long long way. Each precious day. I'm reading Ecclesiastes
And the eye is not filled with seeing.

In a lighter mood, it's hard to beat the bawdy, shaggy-dog humor of
"Another Imaginary Voyage," where rhyming, mock-Kabbalistic
quatrains mull over the reception, by mystical beings, of a sexual
encounter that might have been. (If you guessed that it would end
with a pun about "the world to come," your mind's as dirty as mine,
and we'd both be right.)

In *The Book of Life*, Ostriker has a little suite of poems about Is-
rael and Palestine, most of them from *No Heaven*. A snapshot of
progressive American Jewish ambivalence, they're not her strongest
work, and she herself seems a little uneasy with them. Consider
"Divrei," a two-part poem from *No Heaven* that takes its cue from
the refrain of Jacob Glatstein's famous Holocaust poem "*Nisht di*
meysim loybn got" ("Dead Men Don't Praise God"), "We received
the Torah on Sinai / And at Lublin we gave it back." "At Masada we
gave you our souls / At Auschwitz we took them back," Ostriker
writes, adopting the undeceived stance of a self-defense maven, one
of the Heaven-mistrusting Jews who has "repeated *Never again* and
taught it to our children." Here's the original second stanza:

Oh you who have countless eyes
You whose entire body is eyes, eyes and language
You who say *Not by might and not by power*
Will you stop dreaming, my God
Do you understand nothing?

A fine, heartbroken question: one that underscores the vulnerability
behind the swagger of the first stanza, and that deploys its allusions
with exquisite precision. The italicized tag is Zechariah, a reading
deployed every Hanukkah, per rabbinic instruction, to counter-
point the holiday's military fanfare; to call God a dreamer makes
him a Joseph, or at least one of the young who dream dreams in
Joel; and "nothing" is a word to conjure with, by now, in Ostriker's
oeuvre. *The Book of Life*, however, changes the poem's title to "Di-
vrei: The Settlers," and turns that grand ending to this:

You who promise and promise
Here is our prayer: Bless this fence. Bless this gun.

The phrasing is tighter, more muscular, not least because of the steady rhythm of doublings: "not might" and "not power"; "promise" and "promise"; "promise" and "prayer"; "bless fence" and "bless gun." Yet fences and guns never belonged to "the settlers" alone, nor are they exclusively a post-Holocaust phenomenon. (For a measured corrective, see Anita Shapira's *Land and Power: The Zionist Resort to Force, 1881–1948*.) "Divrei: The Settlers" implies that only those *other* Jews comprise the poem's "we," while the poet and her readers, tender as butter, watch from a distance. There's no mixed dancing allowed.

As Jewish Does

Does a poem have to be about some explicitly Jewish subject to count as, or to be *interesting* as, a "Jewish poem"? The editors of the new *Bloomsbury Anthology of Contemporary Jewish American Poetry*, Deborah Ager and M. E. Silverman, note that they have "included poems that both do and do not focus on Jewish themes," in order to "convey the breadth and depth of Jewish personhood"—this anxious gesture coming ninety-five years after the *In Zikh* manifesto announced that "One does not need any particular 'Jewish themes'" to write a Jewish poem. "A Jew will write about an Indian fertility temple and Japanese Shinto shrines as a Jew," the manifesto continues. "A Jewish poet will be Jewish when he writes poetry about 'Vive la France,' about gratitude to a Christian woman for a kind word, about roses that turn black, about the courier of an old prince, or about the calm that comes only with sleep. It is not the poet's task to seek and show his Jewishness." For "Jewish" you can swap in "Yiddish," since they're the same word in the original—but even in Anglophone poetry, Jewish is as Jewish does, and it's both more fun and more true to see the full range of Ostriker's poems as "Jewish" than to pluck out the few that do what we expect.

Ostriker's two recent collections, *The Book of Seventy* (2009) and *The Old Woman, the Tulip, and the Dog* (2014), open up that repertoire of Jewish doings. Marking Ostriker's arrival at three score years and ten, *The Book of Seventy* opens with an epigraph from Basho ("Barn burned down. Now we can see the moon") and ends with a one-line poem called "Zeno," in which Ostriker asks the Greek philosopher whether she has finally grown "transparent enough." Given this frame, you might expect the poems in between to hanker after both vision and contemplative calm, and early in the book, in "Approaching Seventy," Ostriker does her best to imagine those ideals:

> Please, I thought, when I first saw the paintings
> de Kooning did when Alzheimer's had taken him
> into its arms and he could do nothing
>
> but paint, purely paint, transparent, please let me
> make beauty like that, sometime, like an infant
> that can only cry
>
> and suckle, and shit, and sleep,
> boneless, unaware, happy
> brush in hand no ego there he went

Yet as the book goes on, the "weirdly old" poet who declares that she has "less interfering with my gaze now / what I see I see clearly" turns that gaze on too many messy, freshly imagined things—including herself—to stay for long in any state of egoless bliss. Despite "red neon EXIT signs everywhere," or perhaps because of them, she keeps trying on new voices, some tough-minded and clinical (a dying housefly, a surgeon, a disgusted patriot looking at pictures of Abu Ghraib), some loving well what they might leave ere long.

The most interesting poems to consider as *Jewish* are in the book's central frieze of poems about, or spoken by, an assortment of deities. The supplication poem called "Kol Nidre" in *The Book of Life*—here it's called "Prayer in Autumn"—nestles among verses envisioning Demeter and Persephone, Artemis and Aphrodite, Kali and Gaia. As Pound says in the lines from "Religio: or, the Child's Guide to Knowledge" that preface the section, "What is a god? / A god is an eternal state of mind." But the state of mind invoked by "Prayer in Autumn" doesn't suit Ostriker particularly well, whether by that we mean the self-abasing state of mind of the poem's speaker or the sulky, judgmental deity it envisions as an addressee. (One winces at its obsequious shuckling: "we promise to love only you / faithful, faithful, we promise // we lie, we are not competent / still we implore you," etc.) "Lord Krishna to the Summer Handyman," by contrast, fits Ostriker like a well-worn sandal, with her lifelong multiplicity taking a new, delightful form:

Whenever you hammer I'm here inside your arm
which to me resembles a 'sixty-five Plymouth,

seedy but comfortable. When like a boy
you go barefoot through the house, completely happy,

I'm the pine floor, the whitewashed
walls and the open windows, I'm also the spiders

and the rush of color outdoors,
I smell like one muddy thing after another.

Late afternoon you're tired, you need a beer
I'm a cold beer hitting your palate

I'm not particular. When
next fall your pretty wife

throws a final fit and walks out,
I'm her too.

Is this a "Jewish poem"? I'd say so: To be a late-twentieth-/early twenty-first-century American Jew entails a certain familiarity with other gods and traditions, and for many of us a nagging, bemused suspicion that someone else's Eternal State of Mind might be rather more chipper and appealing than our own.

Late in *The Book of Seventy*, some local wildflowers aim a plea at the passing poet. "*Aren't you Whitman's daughter?*" they ask. "*Please look at me, please love me.*" The state of mind Ostriker dubs "Lord Krishna" does indeed sound a bit like Lord Whitman to me, but does she herself contain multitudes? As a rule, her selves don't proliferate, but rather come in dialectical pairs: she is and is not a secular Jew; she loves and hates the psalms. However, the first of the deity poems, "The Blessing of the Old Woman, the Tulip, and the Dog," shows Ostriker thinking in threes for a change: three stanzas, three speakers, three takes on what it might mean to be "blessed." Since 2009 she has published several dozen poems featuring this power trio, and these have now been gathered in *The Old Woman, the Tulip, and the Dog*. The book endears itself with a waltzing rhythm. Ostriker introduces a topic and the trio consider it, as in "Awakening":

It can take a lifetime
says the old woman

It can take a single deep kiss
says the tulip

Time to take a nap
says the dog

Or they each react to the same circumstance, like "The Beautiful Morning Triptych":

Oh what a beautiful morning
sang the old woman
striding past the tulip
without looking

Besame, besame mucho
sang the tulip
in a smooth yet throaty voice
like Cesária Évora

Je ne regrette rien
sang the dog
cruising past the tulip
on his leash

Sometimes the three agree in substance but differ in tone; sometimes they argue; and sometimes they just talk past one another, leaving the poem as a whole nicely elusive. You can't miss the irony in the first stanza of "The Beautiful Morning," for example, but what are we to make of the dapper canine in the third? Does he not regret what he did off-leash the night before, or the fact that he's back on it now?

Given her taste for contrariety, Ostriker might simply have presented herself as a woman "of three minds, / Like a tree / In which there are three blackbirds." Why divvy up these states of mind between human, flower, and animal? And why have them speak in this same order all the way through? My first impulse was to map the three onto some kind of conceptual grid: id, ego, and superego; faith, hope, and charity; truth, goodness, and beauty—that sort of thing. In the end, though, the poems seem more convivial than conceptual. Each of these characters may be a split-off and stylized version of Ostriker, but each sticks in mind as a more or less distinctive figure. The old woman, for example, shares Ostriker's activism, righteous anger, and love of religion, at least when the spirit hits, but she's far more fretful, vulnerable, and given to reminiscence. The tulip, by contrast, lives "in the open air and the azure present moment," infatuated by her own allure ("I have been told that I am myself a work of art," she preens, flashing the "up-ended skirt" of her petals) and by the power of eros generally. ("I felt / the earth move under my roots," she sighs after receiving a kiss from the sun.) Where the old woman loves "playing the role of Minerva . . . / teaching the young manners and morals and math," the tulip cares little for such human work. "I sow not / neither do I spin," she reminds us, "but I am arrayed in more glory / than King Solomon / you can read about it," and she tips her hat to Jesus as a "smart young man" who "saw / what I truly / am." The adjective is deftly chosen: to the flower, Christ's perspicacity renders him not wise, good, or moral, but trim, stylish, and dashing.

As for the dog, who gets the last word, he's a social, savoring animal. He loves the "good stinks" of the modern city, and he surges with limbic pleasure when he's with his fellows and pain when shut out. "To be banded together with friends is to be free," he exults as he dreams of the Iditarod; "there was no reason to make me leave the room / or to have pushed the door until it clicked" he whimpers when his owners kick him out of bed. Unlike the old woman and tulip, he has no time for theology—it's "bunk," he scoffs, "but the springtime wind is real"—though he's happy to muse philosophically as he scratches his balls. Capable of pure, untroubled happiness, he's a handy, shaggy, simplified figure for what *the volcano sequence* variously called "*shakti*," "*shekhinah*," "*spiritus*," and "rapture in the adrenals." In that earlier book, Ostriker portrayed such power as being never entirely moral—"tiger, lamb, tiger / raccoon— // we are that mixed animal / you are that mixed god," she wrote. (The raccoon is her American contribution to Blake's iconic menagerie.) The animal in this new volume likewise bodies forth "energy, leaping and fanged energy," but he's housebroken and mostly genial, despite his talk about what he might do if "unleashed."

The Old Woman, the Tulip, and the Dog may lack the driven, expansive quality of *The Mother / Child Papers* or *the volcano sequence*, and the fierce resolve of *The Book of Seventy*, which opened with a valedictory sigh but rallied, again and again. "Sit and watch the memory disappear / romance disappear the probability / of new adventures disappear," the book began; "Damn right. We are talking about defiance," harrumphs its penultimate line. Yet it's a fascinating addition to Ostriker's body of work as a Jewish poet. Though light on explicitly Jewish content, it often reads like one of those passages in the Talmud or Zohar where, so to speak, illustrious rabbis show up at the sandbox for some parallel textual play. And its shifting dicta nicely embody the skeptical, carnal Jewishness that Ostriker has always striven to capture. Once she associated such Jewishness with *Yiddishkeit*, Ginsberg, and family drama, but now the Biblical character known as Qoheleth ("the Preacher") seems to strike her as a more compelling model. This least deceived of men careers between contrasting moods and clashing admonishments—indeed, as the Talmud notes, "the Sages wished to hide the Book of Ecclesiastes, because its words are self-contradictory" (*Sabbath* 30b). "No wonder I find him delightful," Ostriker writes in "Ecclesiastes as Witness," the central essay in *For the Love of God*. She likes the way Qoheleth "records these contraries without choosing between them" and teaches us "to slide . . . from bitterness through pathos into laughter, and out into peace," his grim wit giving way not just to "bemused compassion" but to delectation and gusto. (Remember "eat, drink, and be merry"? That's straight out of Qoheleth's mouth, in the King James Bible.)

It seems right and just, then, and not simply clever, that a moment after Ostriker's tulip quotes that "smart young man" Jesus to praise her own glory, her mutt struts his stuff to a tune from the Preacher, albeit with a Memphis twist:

> I ain't nothing but a hound dog
> cryin' all the time
> nothin'
> but a hound dog cryin'
> said the dog
> but the preacher says
> no matter
> how blue I may get
> I am a damn sight better
> than a dead lion

In the stained glass windows of my Other Synagogue, he romps among the iconography: the Lion of Judah, the Serpent of Dan, the Deer of Naftali, the Dog of Alicia.

MARILYN KRYSL

On *For the Love of God: The Bible*
as an Open Book

A major American poet and critic twice a finalist for a National
Book Award, Alicia Ostriker is also an inveterate reader of scripture.
She has engaged the Bible in two works of literary, cultural criti-
cism, *Dancing at the Devil's Party* and *The Nakedness of the Fathers*. In
For the Love of God she addresses six of the Hebrew Bible's books—
the Song of Songs, the book of Ruth, Psalms, Ecclesiastes, Jonah,
and Job—and interprets them as counter-texts that resist the Bible's
dominant structures of authority. From my description you might
imagine the book as the usual critical analysis of text, but Ostriker
is not the typical critic. She is a poet, and demands that critical prose
deliver what poetry delivers: the verbal passion of intense emotional
engagement.

Her method is daring. Imagine a work of scholarship in which
the writer talks about the Hebrew Bible as one talks of a living
person full of human contradictions and with an emotional agenda.
Of the text she says this: "It is sexual and skeptical, just as I am." She
speaks of it as of an acquaintance of long standing who takes an
interest in her. "It seems to want me to live more intensely" (4).
Thus we are invited to partake of a fierce and gentle wrangling
between Ostriker and her pal/lover/antagonist, the text—in which
talking to the text becomes synonymous with talking to God him-
self. And in addition she has the chutzpah to offer him, generously,
the intimacy of her self-revelatory attention.

Theirs is an intimate conversation, for Ostriker is both passionate
advocate of this text and fierce critic. The Song of Songs, for in-
stance, has been construed by others as an allegory of the love be-
tween God and Israel. But the Song "is radical," Ostriker writes,
because it fuses the physical and spiritual, and portrays an assertive
woman whose lover is neither her subordinate nor her superior
(18). Ostriker posits the lovers' equality as a model for the relation
between God and human beings. "What I have written," she says,
"will seem absurd. . . . God as the lover equal to the self? God as the

lover who takes no interest in control or dominance but only in delight? . . . Impossible. And very much more impossible if we are women" (28).

She brings a nuanced cultural awareness to bear when she engages Ecclesiastes's Qoheleth. "He is like a Wall Street tycoon or a media celebrity," she says, "facing the grim reaper." And "in what was probably a third-century BCE Palestine under Ptolemaic rule, Qoheleth inhabited a world like ours, dominated by the marketplace. His profit motif is our profit motive. If he is cynical, his cynicism should sound familiar to us" (83). The conversation between Ostriker and Qoheleth also reads in places like a confab between two women friends divulging self-doubt, longing, and anger. "When I am miserable," Ostriker writes, "I want the moment to go away, but it clings tenaciously, or more accurately I wrap it stubbornly around myself like a winter coat. I brood that nobody loves me. . . . but the truth is I do not deserve to be loved: I'm a bad mother, daughter, teacher, friend, citizen. I don't do enough to help erase poverty, injustice, and war. I am incompetent, stupid, a failure. Or alternatively I am brilliant and unappreciated. . . . And so on. Around the loop." She then hears in Qoheleth's remarks her own response to this self-interrogation. "I hear Qoheleth laughing at himself. He laughs at the joke of having a self that inevitably ties itself into knots" (87–88).

Ostriker's wrestling with the Psalms addresses the fear we project outward as anger against the other. We become the self-righteous voice in Psalm 137, a self that makes the predictable, furious vow: I may be in exile now, but I will never forget, and one day I will take revenge—*and happy shall he be, that dasheth thy little ones against the stones.* "What I recognize in the poem," she writes, "is my resistance to a God who deals cruelly with us and still demands our praise" (73). In response she writes a poem to God portraying him as a partner/pal/lover who's betrayed her trust.

> I am not lyric any more
> I will not play the harp
> for your pleasure. . . .
>
> I will not kill for you
> I will never love you again
>
> unless you ask me (72)

The satisfaction and pleasure this work delivers could not have happened without Ostriker's confident and self-revelatory candor. "When I read the Song of Songs," she writes, "I am in love again for the first time, body and soul are fused, and the world is holy." The Psalms are "white hot poems" that "go straight to the limbic system." And when she reads Ecclesiastes, she remarks, "I am intellectually exhilarated and feel capable of achieving serenity" (144–45). On goes her articulation of our intimate engagement with this religious text. "When I read Jonah I come face to face with my depressive and suicidal impulses, and when I read Job I am the descendent of East European Jews who thought it was up to them to make the world a better place" (145).

Ostriker is just as fascinating when she turns to exegesis, as in her discussion of the subtly layered Hebrew term *hevel*. The King James Bible translates this as "vanity." But *hevel* also "may mean 'vapor' or 'mist,' with a connotation of 'breath,' and so a suggestion simultaneously of that which is essential to life, and that which is utterly ephemeral." And *hevel*, she writes, "may mean 'wind.' It may mean 'emptiness' or 'void,' in a sense adjacent to Taoist or Buddhist concepts of emptiness." *Hevel* is not quite vanity "though close. As close as a breath." Hence the remark: "I have seen all the works that are done under the sun, all *hevel* and a striving after wind." "All human effort," Ostriker summarizes, "is an effort to control the wind, to control the spirit, the Witness says." Thus "we may find a door that, when passed through, opens straight into the existentialism of Camus" (79–80).

For the Love of God concludes with Ostriker's take on the book of Job. God imagines he's supplied restitution by giving Job ten new sons and daughters to replace those God killed. But God apparently has little knowledge of a pregnant woman's labor, birthing, and nurturing of children. "But when I think of the supposedly happy ending, in which Job has ten nice new sons and daughters to replace the ones God killed off in a bet, I feel I am hearing a scream thousands of years old, or as if that scream inhabits my own throat. . . . To me, the reparation offered . . . is obscene. I imagine that one day Job's wife (that is to say, collective womankind) will gather the *chutzpah* to question God the way Abraham did, the way Jeremiah did, the way her husband did. I try to imagine her confrontation with God and what she demands as reparation" (136).

You want this book because it's the elegant, profound version of *The Old Testament for Dummies*. And you want it especially because

Ostriker herself is extraordinary. Think again of her remark that the Hebrew Bible "seems to want me to live more intensely." Her engagement with these counter-texts enables her—and us—to achieve that quantum leap. Of the text she writes, "I can wrestle with it. It fights back, and we both grow stronger" (144).

WESLEY MCNAIR

The Transformation of Grief in "Elegy Before the War"

Anyone who has experienced the shock of grief will recognize the disjointed thought process in the opening section of Alicia Ostriker's extraordinary poem, "Elegy Before the War." Days after the death of her mother, Ostriker is bringing her back through photographs, remembering how she looked in the hospice bed, stunned all over again by her mother's final silence, and insisting that she return. *She is dead, she is alive, she is dying, she cannot be gone.*

The discontinuous process of thought in the poem's first section is linked with a keenly felt and startling description.

> How small and frightened she was in her hospice bed,
> How light abandoned the hopeful gaze,
>
> How the mouth gap with its gurgle from the sad
> Lungs made us feel like Moses, made to see
> God's backside from a cleft in the rock,
>
> The mystery diminished not one grain,
> The face and hands outside the cotton quilt
> Soft, horrible, fine—

Moved as we are by Ostriker's response to her mother's dying and death, we may not see that section I introduces us to the methodology of the poem in general. "My writing is always a gamble," Ostriker said in an interview published in the *Dallas Review*. "I take the risk of going deep into myself, trusting that if I can go deeply enough, and translate the complex of feelings within myself into articulate language, it will be meaningful to others. . . . I like a poem to have a feel of improvisation about it." Such improvisation is clearly evident in "Elegy Before the War." The difference is that through her grief in this poem she goes deeper into her feeling life than ever before, breaking through rational thought to an intuitive and imaginative way of thinking that is unusual even for her. The leaps of that thinking present an argument derived from section I, concerning the horror of death, the preciousness of human life, and the value of love and hope.

Important to note is the alternative mode of thought in "Elegy Before the War" that undermines the "rational" justifications of the poem's enemies, the war-makers of Israel and Palestine, and of the United States in the run-up to the Iraq war. Ostriker is out to expose the truth behind their high-sounding justifications for violence and destruction. But she starts with the simpler truth of her own personal despair, resulting first from her mother's death, then from the world situation of 2002–2003, the one distress leading quickly to the other. As she put it in her *Dallas Review* interview, "the poem took off like a runaway horse almost as soon as it began." What's exciting for a reader in the poem's opening is that she herself doesn't quite seem to know where she is going from one intuitive jump to the next, moving in section II from what had seemed to be the subject of the elegy, her mother, to images of a "spiritually arid" desert and invocations of poets from the past.

Gradually, as we participate in the poem's creation, we learn to trust its leaps and associations. We discover that the desert alludes to the Middle East, especially Iraq, and that Ostriker invokes the four poets—all visionaries who were themselves opposed to violence—for courage as she seeks a voice to counter war's destructive power and address its American advocates, imaged as "Greedy teeth" that "smile at the microphone" and "know where the oil is." Yet the restless, unpredictable poem will not allow us the complacency of our conclusions. For at the end of section II, just when we have settled on who the enemy is, Ostriker abruptly sides with "our friends, Israel and Palestine," drinking to them and noting how much she—and we—enjoy the images

> Of cruel death in the newspaper and on the screen.
> They taste good. I like them. You like them. They are their own
> Best advertisement. We like to shudder at them. We like to blame.

This unsettling turn is one of the poem's most brilliant, suggesting that in our search for those who are responsible for war's destruction we must not overlook ourselves.

Nor should we overlook the poverty-stricken citizens around us, who are the sure evidence of a failed social contract, ignored during peacetime, conscripted during war. Thus, Ostriker devotes section III to a description of the poor people who live next door. Lying in the dark of springtime, without the comfort of her parent or her country, she makes "inaudible orphan sounds," then hears orphan sounds from the neighboring house, where "bedsheets hang in the windows instead of drapes": a man's "chronic, unstoppable cough" and his wife's coaxing of their dog: "*Gypsy. Stop it. Come here. / Good girl, good girl.*" Ostriker concludes the section by determining to make "music of that." Through her simple and affecting description, however, she has already done so.

The juxtaposition of that scene and section IV is dramatic, for the new section features two poets of wit who would never have written a poem of compassion for the poor, nor tried to change the minds and hearts of readers through it. W. H. Auden famously wrote that poetry "makes nothing happen," and his companion, James Merrill, believed that only the form of a poem mattered, not its content. Therefore, Ostriker imagines the two of them sharing "a contest of puns / Over in the heaven of the deserving ones." Section IV consists of a single rhymed quatrain, and its brevity and formalism provide the finishing touch of her satire, suggesting the order and emptiness of art for art's sake.

In section V, Ostriker steps back into the main argument of her poem, now taking on America as it prepares for its war in Iraq. Where, she wants to know, does this "impulse to destroy / This need for an enemy" come from? As befits the poem, she deals with the question through startling shifts of tone and approach. The section moves from an earnest questioning ("Dear animal inside us whom in other respects / We cherish, is it you?") to a parody of the American success story, in which the impulse-to-destroy climbs the ladder of DNA to serve on a corporate board of directors; to jokes about capitalism and communism that show the brutality of each; to gibes ("The trouble with America / Is she is a big bully // And a big coward, / Also that she has no conscience"). Then she brings the guitarist Jimi Hendrix into her poem, recalling his antiwar version of the "Star Spangled Banner" at Woodstock, "Like a cry of absolutely / Pained rage, a train jumping its tracks."

Yet the most dramatic shift comes next, a direct address of any American reader who despite the poem is still attracted to "ignorant violence that stunts, / Stints, stains, struts, standardizes, brutally strangles / The intelligence." How to handle such recalcitrance? Ostriker calls for some anti-American jokes, but the comedians are

"Tucked in their cages / Like tame monkeys" (one thinks of late-night TV comics with their multimillion-dollar contracts). Then she asks America's accountants to "save us / From the mudslide of dollars." The irony of each plea is profound and trenchant, and through it, Ostriker makes her final attempt in section V to get her readers' attention.

But her irony continues in the four lines of section VI, where she reprises the theme of artists and art—in this case, calendar art in America, which ignores not only the impulse toward violence and war-making, but history itself.

> Blessed be the watercolorists
> Who do normal mediocre meadows and lakes
> As if the twentieth century had never occurred
> And blessed be whoever buys their paintings.

Short as this ironic blessing is, its meaning is complex. Its original source, the seventh verse of the Beatitudes ("Blessed are the peacemakers / for they are the children of God") refers not to those who offer the peace of denial, like the watercolorists, but to those who bring conflict to an end by facing and understanding the forces that have caused it. Such peacemaking is for Ostriker crucial to the poem at hand and to art's mission in general. The alternative she describes is not art at all but escapism, supporting the fantasies of its consumers.

In the final section of "Elegy Before the War" she returns to the original subject of the poem, her mother, who is now quite different from the figure of section I. For, having conducted her poetic struggle against war and its perpetrators, Ostriker is able to see her mother as a kind of hero, a fighter for social justice and her first teacher in the ways of peace.

> When I was young, she taught me not to hit or hate
> Anybody, she thought education was the answer, she said most people
>   Were ignorant and superstitious but not us.

Was her mother's growing madness in later life influenced by the madness of America, the "land of bankers and lynch mobs / In her girlhood, land of brokers and bombs at her death"? Ostriker offers no answer to this line of speculation, but as she moves toward the end of her poem, one thing is clear: she does not so much mourn the death of the old woman in section VII as the death of the young woman who once taught her to struggle against the world's evils, "my hopeful young mother, / My mother who promised we would overcome / the bosses and bigots." It is she Ostriker longs for at the end of her poem: "I want her, I want her // To come back and try again."

This final wish seems the more poignant because it can never be realized; after all, no one can now bring her mother back. Yet I believe that the wish has been realized by "Elegy Before the War" itself. For in this remarkable poem, the most important to come out of America's war in Iraq, Alicia Ostriker becomes the very woman she longs for, trying again on her mother's behalf. The better world her mother fought for may have been denied to her during her lifetime, but the poem derived from her example will now live on with its own hope for a better world, offering future readers all they might need for inspiration and encouragement.

TOI DERRICOTTE

Writing Like an Old, Wise, Mature Poet
It's Okay to Play and Joy Is Political

I met Alicia Ostriker forty-five years ago. We belonged to a circle of poets called Poets and Writers of New Jersey. We were in our thirties and had just started being public poets. I can tell you that she was one of the most beautiful women I had ever seen, with thick long rich hair that she wore in an elegant chignon. She had a strong chin and jaw line, a perfect nose, and her profile sometimes tilted up in a little slant when she was quiet and attentively listening—which reminded me of Stanley Kunitz—so that she had a little bit of that look of an aristocrat. She was feeling herself through this new society of poets—as I was. She was a Blake scholar, she taught at the university; I was one of the first teachers in the New Jersey Poets in the School program. I had always been intimidated by real college teachers, scholars, but soon we found kinship in the kind of poetry we wanted to write—and I found out she too was a bit insecure. We both wanted to tell the truth until something broke, something in us first, in our hearts, but since our hearts are a space in the world, it opened up a little space in the world that had been closed for others too. To see her face crack open with girlish laughter and friendship has always been a great pleasure. She has a ferocious appetite for everything that is to be appreciated—motherhood, sex, food, dogs, and girlfriends. And I've seen more and more ferocious joy come over forty and more years. The shadow that occluded seems to be no longer a demon, but rather a now-and-then visitor who shows up like an old friend just to say hi.

We both wrote our female poems, both wrote our pregnancy and birth poems. We cheered each other on, we gloried with books and children, we suffered in love, we supported each other when we couldn't support ourselves, when we thought we were worthless.

We always told each other that the personal is political when we wrote those fearful poems of shame and self-revelation. I felt we were hammering at the walls of secrecy and abuse. I say in *The Black Notebooks* that racism attempts to assault the very idea of the self, to deal a shattering blow to the center of all thought, the self as perception. I ask, "Isn't that racism's greatest injury?" The poem goes down into that broken center and speaks to it: you're all right. It attests to the worth of the self, to a space where the self is not invaded constantly by another's will and projected self-hate, where the self is safe to be. This is a self that begins in pleasure.

I would like to share the first of three sections of a poem by Alicia that brings raw self confronting truth together with a joyous appetite for life, a poem called, "Approaching Seventy." By the way, I like very much that thoughtful serious word "approaching"; it is a word a warrior or monk might use. You don't go quickly, and you don't sneak up on it either, you walk toward it standing straight, looking it straight in the eye, respectful, as you might walk toward a person of high rank. Seventy is a big and awesome thing!

I hope you don't mind, but I'm going to notice some things about the poem that I love as I read it.

Sit and watch the memory disappear

I love that the memory is not just disappearing, but she's watching it—and she's not watching it like a movie, outside, she's grown to be a wiser person, bigger than this scary thing that's happening to her that holds her and takes her in.

Sit and watch the memory disappear
romance disappear the probability
of new adventures disappear

There's no punctuation; it's as if she's found the simplest way to speak, a kind of language so direct and clear that it doesn't need little squiggles and interruptions to help you figure things out.

well isn't it beautiful
when the sun goes down
don't we all want to be where we can watch it

You can just hear the tone, her making in-jokes to all of us, the living, those on this side of the earth; she's pulling our leg.

176

redden
sink to a spark
disappear

Six words and she's captured a sunset, but not flat, like a painting, moving, happening, right before our eyes.

redden
sink to a spark
disappear

～

Your friend goes to Sri Lanka and works
for a human rights organization
in the middle of a civil war

where she too might be disappeared any time
and another friend goes to retreats

Notice that she gets in friendship, global politics, and spirituality in five lines, everything most meaningful in her life, just boom, right there in five lines.

sits miserably waiting for ecstasy and ecstasy

actually comes, so many others
so many serial monogamists seeking love
some open doorway some wild furious breath

～

Please, I thought, when I first saw the paintings
de Kooning did when Alzheimer's had taken him
into its arms and he could do nothing

but paint, purely paint, transparent, please let me
make beauty like that, sometime, like an infant
that can only cry,

and suckle, and shit, and sleep,
boneless, unaware, happy,
brush in hand no ego there he went

So poignant, so small in the number of words, one line "Brush in hand no ego there he went," so great in its implication—pay attention, it all goes so quickly.

~

A field of cerise, another of lime
a big curve slashes across canvas
then another and here it is the lucidity

each of us secretly longs for
as if everything belonging to the other world
that we forget at birth is finally flooding

back to the man like a cold hissing tide
combers unrolling while he waits on the shore
of the sandy canvas brush in hand it comes

There it is, in her own work now, that lucidity for which she praises the painter, that short-cut to the greatest truth. She's worked her whole life for this gift.

~

So come on, gorgeous, get yourself over
to the sandy shore with the sleeping gulls
—does the tide rise or doesn't it

and are you or are you not willing
to rise from sleep, yes, in the dark, and patiently
go outside and wait for it

and do you know what is meant by patience
do you know what is meant by going outside
do you know what is meant by the tide?

Rumi loves her for her wisdom about and acceptance of human nature, and for her ability to laugh.

As she's gotten older, that joy has become more intense, more whittled down and defined, refined, more integral in the language, in her work there is a wild and revolutionary expression of joy—revolutionary because we don't see it expressed in many other poets' work, men or women, and also, because joy is one of the first things tamped down by the killers of our humanity. Alicia, our teacher, tells us to be brave, to show the tenderest part. Joy is an act of resistance.

AFAA MICHAEL WEAVER

Waiting for the Light

Waiting for the Light is a place. It is a question. It is a place where questions are tossed into the air to fly away, like overfed pigeons so that the Poet can savor a raw acceptance of the city. It is Alicia Ostriker's new book. It is a hard testament into which we can speak as responses to her call, or as the querulous hands adding to the Midrash, scribbling and wondering. In the title poem to her new book, the Poet speaks to the late Frank O'Hara. She asks the question many of us might ask, that of what it all comes to and where it is going. If O'Hara were to answer from the place he inhabits, a place of light, the origin of light, or the freedom from the need for light, he might have interesting things to say about the world of the living.

Throughout her new book, Alicia explains how *Waiting for the Light* as place is "a window looking out / not at a paradise but as a paradise / might be." Now the ever-deepening poet of prescience, she walks in the adornment of language through cities like New York, and the idea of cities as the emblem of what human beings are and can be.

The city is Jerusalem with its walls of infinite layering of history, or Portland, Oregon, famous for, among other things, *Portlandia*, the funny rendering of the end of perfection. Heisenberg's uncertainty principle be what it may, Alicia shows us the reality of deepest compassion, one that takes a comfortable rooting in the uncertainty of knowing anything beyond a commitment to love. More to the point, she gives us poetry itself as incarnated in the hand and gesture of grandly affirming the tradition of the art as it continually emerges from the spoken to the written and back to the spoken again, as the listening and reading audiences' reflections form the accumulated commentary on the single works of a poet and what I hesitantly call the art's tradition.

In a recent talk on eros and metaphor, Alicia evoked the world as full of little bits of possibilities for love, tiny bits of metaphor like Tootsie Roll candies all wrapped up and soaking in the light of suns and moons, waiting to become the transformative energy of love.

She looks out on the idea of the city and on the city itself, New York and elsewhere, and in the global landscape finds a point of equilibrium, where there is joy, where there is celebration, where there is despair. It is the continual flux of change. What else is there, we might ask, as does Alicia when she steps out into the space of what we see but do not know, to inhabit ambiguity as a foundation for a faith in our ability to make ourselves better than we are, and thus relieve ourselves of the need for air support from the invisible world.

"I am slipping through a flaw in time." she explains to O'Hara, and we might think of the moment in "The Day Lady Died" when O'Hara noticed everything around him, all the tiny bits of nothingness and fullness, on the day Billie Holiday's death stood pasted in the headlines. Even as she stands on something as solid as the corner, waiting for the light to change, she stands also on the tentative nature of all things. It is the wisdom of resonance. It is the surety of humor. It is the courage of skepticism and a healthy fear of decency on anything other than the best efforts we human beings can make, as she speaks beyond the veil to Maxine Kumin in "The Redeemed World," that in the world redeemed "the Red Sox will always win."

Alicia continues her dialogue with the invisible via O'Hara to say, "I feel / rather acutely alive but I need a thing of beauty / or a theory of beauty to reconcile me." As the poet addressing the world with a definite hope and addressing poets and poetry with both the accumulated and collective sigh of all of us, Alicia gives us the book of poems as both thing and place. In her reading at St. Francis College for the Women's Poetry Initiative on March 26, 2015, she proclaimed, "a poem is not really a poem until it exists with a voice and until it exists in relation to an audience."

The book of poems as both thing and place in conjunction with the poem inhabited by the voice in relationship with the audience becomes the thing of beauty with which Alicia aligns herself. It is the affirmation of the belief in the word, the deed, the life of the poet concerned more with the world than with herself, and in so doing peeping into the place beyond time and space where we might imagine light lives without a need for light.

Once upon a time I stood on a corner with the poet. It was where late evening approaches the cusp between itself and the night. As we say, night was approaching. We stood looking out on a sheet of ice, or rather what we assumed was a sheet of ice, the real thing known as black ice, and neither of us wanted to fall. But I took on the face of my inheritance, a definite southern patriarchally aligned kindness to women known in some places as chauvinism. "Alicia, wait here for me. We don't need for both of us to fall." She smiled and waited, as I let go of her hand to test the pavement in front of us, me a black man in his early sixties with very little cartilage in one knee and none in the other. She a Jewish woman senior to me, apparently much more spry than I am, and certainly more confident in her abilities on the ice. Let us just say she indulged me, whether that's true or not, but each one of us knows that all is uncertainty, as in the title poem she explains to O'Hara that she wants for millions of others at the corner. The corner is the jumping-off point to head to work or home from work, or to dinner, or to the play being performed across the street, or to any civil movement of human beings where there is civility. For places where civility has fallen apart to admit the entry of war, despairs, and chaos, the poet waits with a saddened heart made stronger and wiser with a belief in what is in front of her eyes as well as what lies vibrantly in her heart. It is hope with all its maddening faults.

In her chapter on the book of Ecclesiastes in *For the Love of God*, Alicia explains that "existence is God's mystery, that life is God's gift, and that 'God' is the name for everything I cannot understand" (98). So it is that "waiting for the light feels like forever." Alicia shows the reader light as the slippery breath of some kind of grace, thus enlightening my inner recovering Baptist scratching the door to nondualistic being in order to believe.

ELEANOR WILNER

It happened this way
Awakening with Alicia Ostriker

It happened this way, some thirty years ago, in a reverie, in that else-
where of Greek myth that is the Dreamtime of the West. I saw, in
the strange clarity of waking vision, a figure overhead, darkening
the day. As it neared, I saw it was the great horse Pegasus descending
from the sky, a huge figure, coming down as if from its own weight,
and gravity's insistence. When it landed, I could see that it was
broken-winged and wounded—terribly, mortally—and it dragged
itself into a nearby cave, and disappeared into the dark. Almost at
once, from the same cave mouth into which it vanished, a figure
emerged: a tall woman, a nimbus of light around her head, a light
that seemed to writhe; it was a living halo: a gleaming mass of waves,
reflecting sun, or its own source of light: impossible to say. And then,
the vision widened—on the rocky slopes around the cave were
figures made of stone—statues as silent, fixed, immobile as the stony
slope on which they stood. I realized then that this was the lair of
the Medusa—and even as this recognition dawned, she looked at
them with a green-eyed gaze, intent on them till they returned her
gaze, and they began to move, the stone to warm, blood to course
in what had been marble veins, and all these figures, as if stepping
out of a paralyzing dream, were, before my eyes, transformed to
breathing flesh.

Now, among the oddities of this vision, which reversed an an-
cient paralyzing spell, was another reversal: the figures restored to
full life and mobility, were not, as in the old Medusa myth, the os-
sified figures of heroic men who had come to slay her, but they
were ourselves—women who, in some essential way, had shared her
fate: out of the male fear of the power of women, and of nature
(which they associated with us, and for which she was emblematic);
like her, we had been turned into mere bodies, deprived of voice
and (as far as possible) of autonomous intellect, divided from our-
selves, and, by social definition, essentially immobilized in an un-
chosen state of sessility. I like that word, sessility, partly for its sug-

gestive sound, and because it denotes the state deriving from the botanist's word <u>sessile</u>: referring to leaves that have no stems, attached directly to the branch or other base; in anatomy: permanently fixed, immobile. I read somewhere that men dream of falling, women of being rooted to the ground. As Muriel Rukeyser wrote, in the poem "Waiting for Icarus," speaking in the invented voice of his lover pacing the beach: "I have been waiting all day, or perhaps longer. / I would have liked to try those wings myself. / It would have been better than this."

Since that time, when this reborn Medusa seemed only an idiosyncratic vision, though one that I was going to be impelled to investigate, I have found myself among such a lively company of women, writers and scholars, the stony years all but forgotten—a company that back then I could only imagine. It is all so recent, and yet I think we have become almost inured to the wonder of it. It was newly brought home to me when I attended a remarkable conference in 2002 in Palermo, called "*Ladre di linguaggi, Il mito nell'immaginario femminile*"—which translates (pretty obviously) as "Thieves of Language, Myth in Women's Imaginary." The convener of this gathering of women scholars and poets, Prof. Eleonora Chiavetta, had named the occasion after the title of the chapter about women poets and revisionist mythology in Alicia Ostriker's *Stealing the Language*, her chapter title a reprise of Claudine Hermann's *Le voleuses de langue*. Eleonora carried about with her Alicia's book, as source and touchstone—a book that was like that enlivening Medusa's gaze—giving us back ourselves—an awakened, embodied community, one that had relocated the sacred meanings and reclaimed its head.

That conference reawakened for me the excitement of women having come so far, so fast. This was, for the University of Palermo, something new: the first such all-women conference, and its participants were women professors from Palermo's university and from universities in Milano, Bologna, and Napoli, from Athens, Trieste, and Smyrna. And the three poets, advertised as "flesh and blood thieves of language," were Mimi Khalvati, Iranian-born but British since early childhood, rewriting Sufi mythology; Sujata Bhatt, from India and later America, now living in Germany—first woman in a long line of writers in her family; and myself—exemplar of that joke I first heard, I think, from Alicia: "what is the difference between a butcher and a poet?" The answer: "two generations."

But the difference between a butcher and a woman poet is precisely the *right* two generations. Which is meant to remind us again of the unlikeliness, given human history in general, and Western history in particular, of being in this lucky generation, and feeling it anew at the gathering in Palermo, the sense of celebration and camaraderie, strengthened in the Sicilian setting, where women had so long been cloistered in the house of silence, and for whom, as Eleonora put it, we were breaking into the house of language, to return it to them.

I have never been in a more congenial group, where the sense of a shared endeavor overcame so entirely the shabbier aspects of academia, and where pettiness, point-scoring, and pretension had been banned from the feast. I am not idealizing here, and if you think I am, it might be a sign that American women's academic progress has been a little too good, and has forgotten its origins. I admit that I worry about this, as I agree with Virginia Woolf that, as we take on the roles to which our gifts and passions direct us, we must remain a little what we were: the Outsider, in order to keep an eye on ourselves. I fear the loss of that perceptive edge.

And while we are remembering, it seems to me necessary to recall how the multiple instances of the way women's experience and vision radically transform the partial myths of the past—knowledge of which we have come to take for granted—how these were first put together for us in that ground-breaking book, Alicia's *Stealing the Language*. In her introduction to the Palermo conference, Eleonora spoke of her debt to that book, quoting Alicia on the necessity to reexamine and recreate the myths that have been codified and transmitted by a canon that has excluded the voices of women, to draw on the powers of the language of tradition to liberate us from its hold, to be like Prometheus and steal our fire from the gods, or rather from those who defined the gods in their own image.

While Alicia's study analyzed the work of American poets, the Palermo conference included women's rewritings of canonical myths without distinction of historical period, literary genre, language, or country of origin. Though given our Italian setting and predominantly Italian cast of speakers, it wasn't surprising that mainly Greek mythic figures recurred—among others—in a plurality of subversive guises, ranging from British playwright Sarah Kane's brutal, nihilist Phaedra and Margarita Liberaki's film version of Phaedra as a mirror of contemporary Greek society; to the subverted Psyche myth in a Eudora Welty novel; to Indian novelists who, like their mythic ancestor, Shaharazad, tell stories to save their lives; to the creation of an androgynous figure from an unlikely meld of Orpheus and Athena in the work of German poet Ingeborg Bachmann; Jocasta, recast as taboo-breaking speaker in a play by Belgian Michèle Fabien, and, in a work by Mexican writer Angelina Muñiz, a Jocasta who refuses guilt and embraces her incest; Penelope reinvented ("O goddess, make him not return") in contemporary Italian women's novels; and so on through twenty-seven presenters in English or Italian (some of whom I could actually follow). I won't mention the food, as Sicilian food and hospitality are beyond description; you had to be there.

But overall, the feeling was one of abundance—a kind of harvest festival (and the conference was in early November): a gathering of the sheaves, so much reinvention of self and world by women, and because—when you deal with myth—you shake the foundations within and without, the theft of that Promethean fire is one that is, inevitably, a political challenge, an undermining of the sanctions of old arrangements and authorities. And the new Medusa, and the long investigation of that vision that had led me to the work of so many women who had been simultaneously having the same dream, though we had never met, and that I had brought as my contribution to Palermo—that Medusa met the older one, the ancient, pre-Olympian power figure on the flag of Sicilia, that moved there in the southern breeze, in that great city that had absorbed and outlived the empires of Greece, Rome, Islam, Byzantium; where we mutually mourned our three deadly throwback B's of that moment: Bush, Blair, and Burlesconi, and plotted a world without them. Who could have imagined back then the election of Trump, who would take high office to an abysmally new low?

Tchaikovsky described the sound of the ice breaking up on the bay outside St. Petersburg as the "thunder of the spring." Alicia heard that thunder, recorded it, and was herself part of the spring that broke the ice. She was ever the enemy of what was frozen, the deadliness of dogma's monumental stone, and always a voice of and for the living flow, as in her poem "Stream," which is one of my personal favorites:

With swift delusional energy:
That's how my best student in '67
Described a rushing

Stream, and I have forgotten
Neither the phrase nor his series
Of quick disintegrations over the next

Few years, a river dropping
Down a flight of steps. It wasn't the acid
He dropped in Vietnam did this, it was the people

He dropped,
That is to say he killed,
He and his army buddies, and took

Personally, I knew because his hands shook
If he tried to talk
About it, and then he'd stop

Out of deference to me perhaps:
Young, I had never seen a person's hands
Shaking. Maybe he'd tell

A bitter joke on the nuns
Who raised him in South Jersey,
Mocking their gestures, and then clutch

His body, small and strong
Like my husband's. I recall his tidy mustache,
The braying giggle that confused the other students

Before he dropped out. I recall there is
A difference between illusion
And delusion, the *maya*

That sustains us, flimsy ghosts in a flimsy world,
And the madness
And suffering that destroy us. The stream isn't

Delusional, I say, it represents
A truth, the actual motion of all matter,
All energy in its interior

Secret torrent that's invisible
To my stupid human
Eye, and it is also

The image of those minds
That smash one way, downhill,
Downhill, amid the spray

Of their uncontrollable
Meditations, downhill,
Slowly or swiftly

Without peace, without hope,
Letting themselves be broken, time
After time, by stone

After stone, and I believe the raging,
The flying water is real,
The tons of it, only

I hate the frozen snowfields
It descends from, a delusional
Purity, and the brutal

Rock that rends it,
A delusional
Solidity.

Alicia has always loved Torah, and is part of the first generation of acknowledged Jewish women scholars and writers to create both commentary and midrash, to love and challenge the Fathers from both within and beyond the tent of Abraham; she knows that what is written lives only by what needs constantly still *to be written*. She has unfailingly fought tradition hardening into dogma ("So forget the rabbis and their frozen Law / A rod that likes / Hitting . . ."), and denounced the false idol of tribal partiality that masquerades as righteousness.

Hers has been, from the first, a poetry *engagé*, as the French say— the kind of poetry that Europe assumes is a necessary companion to the delusive madness of history, but that has always been in short supply here in our bemused nation, insulated even (until 9/11) from its own actions in the world, a people whose portrait Alicia draws in a recent poem, "Fix": ". . . at a loss / As if someone pulled the floor out from under them . . ." but uncertain as to what's lost: "The puzzled ones, the Americans [who] go through their lives / Buying what they are told to buy" (*No Heaven*).

For our poets, this includes being told, until quite recently, to buy the line that "political poetry" is a nonstarter, inviting only suspicion and disdain—as if poetry, and one's life, were narrowly personal matters, while politics, history, and war were something extraneous, impossible to take personally. Then, too, there is the present "cool," which fears being caught out in the expression of any strong conviction. But Alicia has always felt the larger world calling within, and has always boldly gone her own way, and set the pace for others with less chutzpah. For what is more personal than history, the unchosen context of our little lives? Reading *Poetry after Auschwitz*, knowing "how sick and sickening people can become," she writes:

> And now I think we are writing the poems before the holocaust.
> Is this not true? We are writing these poems with all our soul,
> It's our writing, it's our wall.

These lines above are from her recent book, *No Heaven*, where private and public history are experienced as inseparable; writing with searing honesty about her mother's death in "Elegy before the War," she is writing in the same breath about history:

> And we burned her and flew to Arizona
> And the tanks roamed Ramallah and Nablus

The first-person speaker's grief and sense of abandonment is matched by that of the larger world:

> . . . These are dry times, orphan times,
> Fear on the wind, anger in the soil. I cannot imagine an appealing
> future for my species,
> Born to violence that steers the intelligence.

And of her mother's rage she asks:

> What drove her crazy, what wasted her beauty and intellect, was it
> America,
> The *goldene medina* just a joke, land of bankers and lynch mobs
> In her girlhood, land of brokers and bombs at her death

> Hammer to which everything is a nail?

And, with Alicia, along with no heaven, always a little leaven:

Here we need a few anti-American jokes.
What are we afraid of?
Where are the comedians

When we need them?
Tucked in their cages
Like tame monkeys.

Untamed and a figure of inflamed outrage, "The cat of dire memory" has been a presence in my own mind since finding it, in 1989, in "The Bride," Alicia's powerful poem on the bloody hemorrhaging in Israel, a subject to which she returns and returns. Here she writes in a tone of darkest irony, and reveals that the secret government of Jerusalem comprises the cats, sisters for whom the violent history of this city, whose too many lovers "are killing for her / Among the stones," offends their animal nature: "the cats / Have a saying: You've seen one corpse, / You've seen them all." And the figure that has lodged in my memory, carrying Alicia's passion and one that so many of us share, is the cat from whom this feline underground is "receiving orders," an icon into which she breathes life:

. . . a small, blackened
Bronze Egyptian cat
In the Rockefeller Museum
Near the Damascus Gate,
The cat of dire memory, whose heart,
The size of an olive, is heavier
Than an iron cannonball.

Heavy because so angry,
So angry.

One of Alicia's favorite texts, which she often quotes, and which is the epigraph to "Tearing the Poem Up and Eating It," is from Exodus 23:9: "You shall not oppress a stranger; for you know the heart of the stranger, for you were strangers in Egypt." These words open the five-part poem in No Heaven for Yitzhak Rabin, prime minister of Israel assassinated in 1995 by a right-wing Jewish Israeli, a fanatic opposed to the Oslo Accords, and to Rabin's peace initiatives toward the Palestinians. The poem is addressed to God, and expresses her doubt, in the face of atrocity, of poetry itself, and of her own strained belief that

> Justice and compassion together
> Pour through the lifeblood of your poem,
> Your book, but tell it to the bloody plaza

Her complicated and often contradictory feelings and the authenticity of them all, as well as the rich variety and depth of her sources, are manifest in this poem, as in so many, in her ability to radically shift tones, to move by swift turns from a mocking irony to a sensual lyric passage, from a terse compression to a luxuriant expressiveness, from plaint to joking, from a conversational plain speech to an in-your-face vernacular to the heightened language of prophetic outcry.

In its final address to God, the poem's indictment is not of one religion or one nation, but of all tribes, religions, and nations that throughout human history have claimed, and continue to claim, divine sanction for murder:

> Those who remember you promised them the land
> > sow it with corpses
> Those who await messiah
> > dream of apocalypse
> > in which their enemies burn—
> I speak of all your countries, my dear God.

At the same time, she refutes the initial impulse to tear up the poem as impotent in the face of such violence; that refutation is in the last line, the verbal naming of its own action: "I speak."

And let this quotation from the poem serve, as well as any, as emblematic of the long and essential political and ethical engagement of Alicia Ostriker, even in the face of near despair:

> —Tearing the poem up and eating it
> Will get me nowhere. Better to burn than to marry
> What demands to be married, what offers its ring
> Of spurious safety, what demands that I sell my birthright
> Of hope and forget to remember the heart of the stranger
> And better to write than to burn
> And best to clear a path for the wind.

Writings by Alicia Ostriker
A Chronological Bibliography of Her Books

Poetry

Songs. New York: Holt, Rinehart, and Winston, 1969.

Once More Out of Darkness. Berkeley, CA: Berkeley Poets' Cooperative, 1974.

A Dream of Springtime. New York: The Smith, 1979.

The Mother/Child Papers. Boston: Beacon Press, 1980; rpt. Pittsburgh: University of Pittsburgh Press, 2009.

A Woman Under the Surface. Princeton: Princeton University Press, 1982.

The Imaginary Lover. Pittsburgh: University of Pittsburgh Press, 1986.

Green Age. Pittsburgh: University of Pittsburgh Press, 1989.

The Crack in Everything. Pittsburgh: University of Pittsburgh Press, 1996.

The Little Space: Poems Selected and New, 1968–1998. Pittsburgh: University of Pittsburgh Press, 1998.

the volcano sequence. Pittsburgh: University of Pittsburgh Press, 2002.

No Heaven. Pittsburgh: University of Pittsburgh Press, 2005.

The Book of Seventy. Pittsburgh: University of Pittsburgh Press, 2009.

At the Revelation Restaurant and Other Poems. Washington, DC: Marick Press, 2010.

The Book of Life: Selected Jewish Poems, 1979–2011. Pittsburgh: University of Pittsburgh Press, 2012.

The Old Woman, the Tulip, and the Dog. Pittsburgh: University of Pittsburgh Press, 2014.

Waiting for the Light. Pittsburgh: University of Pittsburgh Press, 2017.

Criticism and Mixed Genre Writing

Writing Like a Woman. Ann Arbor: University of Michigan Press, 1983.

Stealing the Language: The Emergence of Women's Poetry in America. Boston: Beacon Press, 1987.

Feminist Revision and the Bible: The Unwritten Volume. Cambridge, MA: Blackwell, 1993.

The Nakedness of the Fathers: Biblical Visions and Revisions. New Brunswick, NJ: Rutgers University Press, 1997.

Dancing at the Devil's Party: Essays on Poetry, Politics, and the Erotic. Ann Arbor: University of Michigan Press, 2000.

For the Love of God: The Bible as an Open Book. New Brunswick, NJ: Rutgers University Press, 2009.

Editions

Blake, William. *William Blake: The Complete Poems.* Edited by Alicia Ostriker. New York: Penguin, 1977. Rpt., Penguin Classics, 2004.

Contributors

Toi Derricotte is cofounder, with Cornelius Eady, of the Cave Canem Foundation. She is the author of five collections of poetry, most recently *The Undertaker's Daughter* (2011). Her memoir, *The Black Notebooks*, received the Anisfield-Wolf Book Award for Non-Fiction and was a *New York Times* Notable Book of the Year. She is professor emerita at the University of Pittsburgh and a chancellor of the Academy of American Poets.

Julie R. Enszer is the author of four poetry collections, *Avowed* (2016), *Lilith's Demons* (2015), *Sisterhood* (2013), and *Handmade Love* (2010). Her most recent edited volume, *The Complete Works of Pat Parker* (2016), won the Lambda Literary Award for Lesbian Poetry. Enszer edits and publishes *Sinister Wisdom*, a multicultural lesbian literary and art journal.

Jenny Factor's first volume of poetry, *Unraveling at the Name*, was the 2001 winner of the Hayden Carruth Award, and her work has appeared in more than a dozen anthologies, including *Poetry 180*. Factor serves on the core faculty at Antioch University Los Angeles.

Daisy Fried's books of poetry include *Women's Poetry: Poems and Advice*; *My Brother Is Getting Arrested Again*; and *She Didn't Mean to Do It*, which won the Agnes Lynch Starrett Prize. She is on the board of the National Book Critics Circle and is poetry editor for the literary/political resistance journal *Scoundrel Time*. Fried teaches in the Warren Wilson College MFA Program for Writers and at Villanova University.

Diana Hume George, an essayist, poet, and critic, teaches creative nonfiction in Goucher College's MFA program. She is the author of an essay collection, *The Lonely Other: A Woman Watching America*, and several poetry collections. Her other publications include *A Genesis*, *Koyaanisqatsi*, and *Blake and Freud*. She is a contributing editor for the *Chautauqua Journal* and former codirector for the Chautauqua Writers' Festival.

Marilyn Hacker is the author of numerous books of poems including *A Stranger's Mirror: New and Selected Poems, 1994–2014* (Norton, 2015), essays, and collections of translations of French and Francophone poets. Her awards include the National Book Award, the Lenore Marshall Prize, the American PEN award for poetry in translation, and the international Argana Prize for Poetry from the Beit as-Sh'ir/House of Poetry in Morocco.

Rabbi **Jill Hammer** is Director of Spiritual Education at the Academy for Jewish Religion in Yonkers, NY, and cofounder of the Kohenet Hebrew Priestess Institute. She has written or coauthored several books, including *The Hebrew Priestess: Ancient and New Visions of Jewish Women's Spiritual Leadership*. Both her scholarship and her poetry, stories, and rituals have appeared widely in journals and anthologies.

Tony Hoagland's newest collections of poems are *Recent Changes in the Vernacular* (2017) and *Priest Turned Therapist Treats Fear of God* (2018). He teaches at the University of Houston, and is working on a collection of craft essays. His awards include the Jackson Poetry Prize, the James Laughlin Prize, the Poetry Foundation's Mark Twain Award for humor in American poetry, and the Folger Shakespeare Library's O. B. Hardison, Jr., Prize in recognition of a poet's teaching.

Cynthia Hogue is the author of nine poetry collections, most recently *In June the Labyrinth*; four books of criticism; award-winning translations; and a collaboration with photographer Rebecca Ross that captures eleven survivors' recollections of Hurricane Katrina. Hogue teaches in the MFA program at Arizona State University, where she is the Maxine and Jonathan Marshall Chair in Modern and Contemporary Poetry.

Marilyn Krysl is a poet, fiction writer, and activist. Her book of poetry *Warscape with Lovers* was awarded the Cleveland State University Poetry Center Prize. Her works have appeared widely, including in *The Atlantic*, *The Nation*, and *The Pushcart Prize Anthology*. She has been an artist in residence at the Center for Human Caring, an unarmed bodyguard for Peace Brigade International in Sri Lanka, and a volunteer at Mother Teresa's Kalighat Home for the Destitute and Dying in Calcutta.

Joan Larkin's five poetry collections include *Blue Hanuman* and *My Body: New and Selected Poems*, which received the Publishing Triangle's Audre Lorde Award. A teacher for many decades, Larkin recently served as the Conkling Writer in Residence at Smith College. Her honors include the Lambda Literary Award, the Shelley Memorial Award, and the Academy of American Poets Fellowship for distinguished poetic achievement.

Wesley McNair has served as poet laureate of Maine, and five times on the jury for the Pulitzer Prize in poetry. His nine collections include the recently published volume *The Unfastening*, and *The Lost Child: Ozark Poems*, which won the 2015 PEN New England Award. McNair has received the Theodore Roethke Prize, the Eunice Tietjens Prize from *Poetry Magazine*, and an Emmy Award as scriptwriter for a television series on Robert Frost.

Jacqueline Osherow is Distinguished Professor of English at the University of Utah. She is the author of eight books of poetry, including *Whitehorn*, *Ultimatum from Paradise*, and the forthcoming *My Lookalike at the Krishna Temple*. A number of her poems deal with Jewish texts, tradition, and history. Among many honors, she has received the Witter Bynner Prize from the American Academy and Institute of Arts and Letters and prizes from the Poetry Society of America.

Eric Selinger is professor of English at DePaul University. He is the author of *What Is It Then Between Us? Traditions of Love in American Poetry* and coeditor of the anthologies *Jewish American Poetry: Poems, Commentary, and Reflections* and *Romance Fiction and American Culture: Love as the Practice of Freedom?* He is currently coauthoring a book on reading popular romance as theological fiction.

Martha Nell Smith is Professor of English and Distinguished Scholar-Teacher at the University of Maryland. Coordinator and executive editor of the *Dickinson Electronic Archives*, she serves on the advisory board of Harvard University Press's *Emily Dickinson Archive*, and is a founding member and president of the Emily Dickinson International Society. Her publications include *Emily Dickinson, A User's Guide, Open Me Carefully: Emily Dickinson's Intimate Letters to Susan Dickinson*, and *Emily Dickinson's Correspondences: A Born-Digital Textual Inquiry*. The 2018 award-winning Indie film *Wild Nights with Emily* is dedicated to her for her work in biography and archival research.

Richard Tayson is the author of two books of poems, *The Apprentice of Fever* and *The World Underneath*, and coauthor of a memoir, *Look Up for Yes*. He recently finished *The Lamentations Collector*, a cycle of poems concerning obsession, addiction, and celebrity culture, and is writing a companion memoir, *Alternate Means of Transport: Chance Encounters with Eight Famous Women*. He works as a freelance editor and teaches in the New School's writing program.

Marion Helfer Wajngot is an associate professor of English at Stockholm University. She has published on the works of William Thackeray, George Eliot, and on poet and Bible commentator Alicia Ostriker. Her works include *The Birthright and the Blessing: Narrative as Exegesis in Three of Thackeray's Later Novels*. She has also taught at Uppsala University, Södertörn University, and the Paideia Institute for Jewish studies in Sweden.

Poet, playwright, and translator **Afaa Michael Weaver** is on the poetry faculty of Drew University's MFA program. *Spirit Boxing* is the newest of his fifteen poetry collections. Weaver was a member of Cave Canem's inaugural faculty, and has been a Fulbright Scholar in Taiwan. He has received the Kingsley Tufts Award, the Harlem Book Fair's Phyllis Wheatley Award, and the Beijing Writers Association's Gold Friendship Medal for his work with Chinese poets.

Eleanor Wilner teaches in the MFA Program for Writers at Warren Wilson College. She has written seven collections of poetry, most recently *Tourist in Hell*, responding to the brutality of the twentieth and twenty-first centuries. Her other works include a verse translation of Euripides's *Medea* and *Gathering the Winds*, a critical study of the social role of visionary imagination. Former editor of *The American Poetry Review*, Wilner's awards include a MacArthur Fellowship and the Juniper Prize.

Index